CLASSIC

THE BASICS

This is an engaging introduction which explores the latest thinking about Classical mythology, the history of interpreting myths and the role of myths in cultural tradition, from painting to opera, philosophy, politics, drama, and religion in the modern day. It answers such questions as, what are ancient myths and who invented them; where do gods come from; what makes a hero; how is Classical myth used in the modern world; and what approaches are there to the study of myth?

Featuring further reading and case studies from antiquity to the modern day, this is an essential introduction to the myths which have been a fundamental part of Western culture throughout history.

Richard Martin is Professor in Classics at Stanford University and has twenty-five years' experience in teaching an introduction to Classical mythology to undergraduate students. He is widely published on Homer, Hesiod, Pindar, Aristophanes, Theognis, and other ancient authors and genres in which mythic narration figures prominently.

THE BASICS

Basics titles on related topics:

ANCIENT EGYPT
DONALD P. RYAN

ANCIENT NEAR EAST
DANIEL C. SNELL

ARCHAEOLOGY (THIRD EDITION)
CLIVE GAMBLE

FOLKLORE
SIMON BRONNER

GREEK HISTORY
ROBIN OSBORNE

CLASSICAL MYTHOLOGY
THE BASICS

Richard Martin

Routledge
Taylor & Francis Group

LONDON AND NEW YORK

First published 2016
by Routledge
2 Park Square, Milton Park, Abingdon, Oxon OX14 4RN

and by Routledge
711 Third Avenue, New York, NY 10017

Routledge is an imprint of the Taylor & Francis Group, an informa business

© 2016 Richard Martin

British Library Cataloguing-in-Publication Data
A catalogue record for this book is available from the British Library

Library of Congress Cataloging-in-Publication Data
Martin, Richard P.
Classical mythology / Richard Martin. – First edition.
pages cm. – (The basics)
Includes bibliographical references and index.
1. Mythology, Greek. 2. Mythology, Classical. 3. Myth. 4. Mythology. I. Title.
BL783.M375 2016
292.1'3–dc23
2015034348

ISBN: 978-0-415-71502-7 (hbk)
ISBN: 978-0-415-71503-4 (pbk)
ISBN: 978-1-315-72718-9 (ebk)

Typeset in Bembo
by Swales & Willis Ltd, Exeter, Devon, UK
Printed and bound by CPI Group (UK) Ltd, Croydon, CR0 4YY

CONTENTS

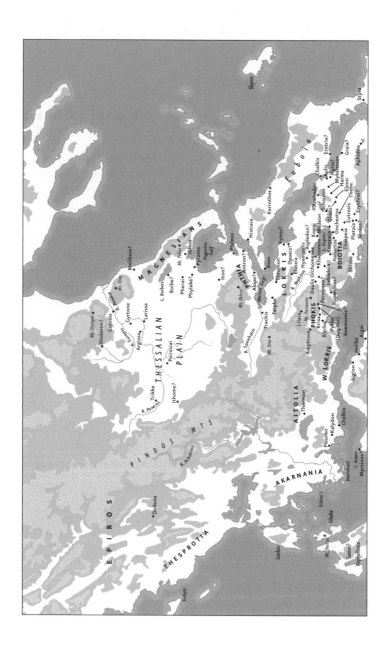

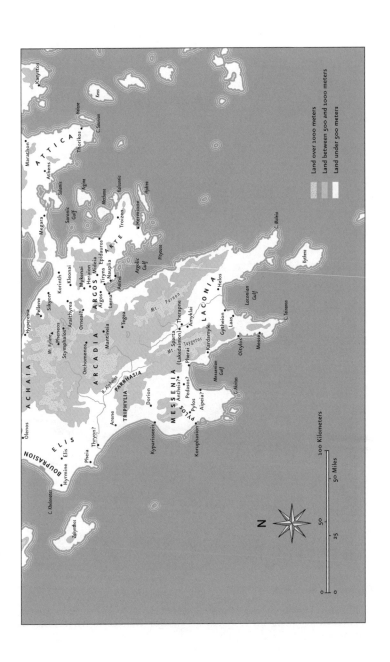

Land over 1000 meters

Land between 500 and 1000 meters

Land under 500 meters

ACHAIA

Olenos

ELIS

BOUPRASION

C. Rheionastos

Hyrmine

Pheia

Elis

Thryon?

Arene

TRIPHYLIA

Kyparisseeis

Dorion

PARRHASIA

R. Alpheios

ARCADIA

Orneai?

Mt. Kyllene

Pheneos

Stymphalos

Orchomenos

Mantineia

Tegea

Hyperesia

Pellene

Sikyon

Araithyrea

Kleonai

Korinth

Mykenai

Heraion

ARGOS

Argos

Mideia

Tiryns

Epidauros

Nauplia

AKTE

Asine

Lerna

Argolic

Gulf

Prigeus

Troizen

Hermione

Methana

Kalaureia

Hydrea

Saronic

Gulf

Aigina

Salamis

Megara

Athens

ATTICA

Marathon

Thorikos

C. Sounion

Helene

Keos

Kanystos

MESSENIA

Antheia?

Pedasos?

Pylos

Aipeia?

Koruphasion

Messenian

Gulf

Aliatsa

Pherai

Mt. Sparta

(Lakedaimon)

Amyklai

Therapne

Mt. Taygetos

Kardamyle

Oitylos

Messe

LACONIA

Mt. Parnon

Helos

Gytheion

Laas

Laconian

Gulf

C. Malea

C. Tainaron

Kythera

N

0   25   50 Miles

0   50   100 Kilometers

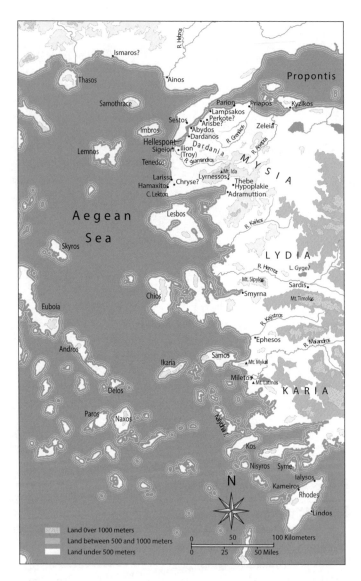

Frontispiece: Sites important in the world of Greek myth

Source: Map of mainland Greece, © International Mapping, from "The Iliad of Homer," trans. Richmond Lattimore, University of Chicago Press 2011. Reproduced with permission.

FIGURES

PREFACE

Classical mythology rapidly draws you into the study of nearly all Western literature, philosophy, art, music, and intellectual history. It does not require advanced knowledge of any one of these, however, to start reading and understanding the tales. This small book attempts to guide the reader to the core elements of ancient Greek and Roman narratives about gods and goddesses, heroes and heroines, while also offering outlines about how the myths shaped culture, and were shaped in turn by more than two thousand years of cultural reception, through artistic responses as well as scholarly analysis.

While the book does not aim to retell or summarize the myths themselves, suggestions are made for sourcebooks that provide such material. The five chapters here build up the context for where and how myths might have begun; how they were transmitted; what meanings have been found in tales of the world's origin, or figures like Oedipus, Heracles, Antigone, Odysseus, and Medea; and what methods, ancient and modern, have yielded fruit in explaining myths whether from the standpoint of psychology or politics. As with any interpretive writing about the Classics, the best an author can hope for is that the reader will turn with wider interest and curiosity to the primary texts that survive from the distant, ancient world.

I have confined Further Reading suggestions to works in English. In transliterating Greek, I have stuck with conventional spellings for familiar names (thus *Oedipus*, not *Oidipous*), but when names are less likely to be well known, I have retained the more authentic forms (mainly -k- instead of -c-; -ai- instead of -ae-; final -os instead of -us).

Richard Martin, San Francisco,
August 2015

1

STORIES THAT STAY

What were ancient "myths" to the people who invented them? This chapter shows how the Greek word that gives us the English "myth" evolved from a term meaning "speech" or "utterance" into something closer to the modern idea, even in the course of the Classical period in Greece (fifth and fourth centuries BC). Myth is put into its broader context of belief and tradition. This in turn will bring us to the growing gap, already seen in the Classical period, between tales like those in Homer and Hesiod and more theoretical ethical thinking. The dissonance led to three major responses by the end of the Classical age: outright rejection; rationalization; and allegorization. Each will be examined in turn. Finally, we'll look at the range of disparate ancient sources from which continuous stories might be woven – or sometimes simply cannot be tied together.

MYTH AS SPEECH

Try this experiment. First, search the internet for the phrase "myth of." What comes up? You might find a few references to characters from ancient Greek stories, like the Myth of Sisyphus (although in one recent search that summoned up an essay by the twentieth-century French writer Albert Camus, giving a philosophical spin to the ancient story of the mortal who was condemned to keep rolling a rock up a hill in Hades for eternity). But most occurrences of the phrase will not be about old Greek tales at all. Among sixty million or so results, you will find books, blogs, or articles titled "The Myth of Multitasking"; "The Myth of Innovation"; "The Myth of American Exceptionalism"; "The Myth of Welfare and Drug Use"; "The Myth of Repressed Memory"; The Myth of Psychotherapy"; and "The Myth of the Rational Voter." There's even "The Myth of Dry Pet Food Cleaning Dog Teeth." Clearly, the only connection among all these is the habit of calling a "myth" something that, despite being a widespread and enduring belief or institution, should be considered (at least in somebody's opinion) fake, false, or faulty. "Myth" in this meaning borders on "common misconception" or, in extreme cases, "big lie."

Now do a search for "mythic." You'll find the adjective attached to heroes, role-playing, adventures and journeys, battles and treasures, creatures, beasts, feats, realms and isles, archetypes (and, yes, an occasional pizza shop). In other words, all the items we associate with exciting, exotic, absorbing sagas, whether Tolkien's *Lord of the Rings* trilogy or the Harry Potter series, can be called "mythic," in an enthusiastically positive sense. No one employing the word like this implies that these things are misconceptions or lies (although almost everyone admits that they are fictions). What is "mythic" is simply not in the same category as what people often call "a myth." How did this split happen and what can the schizoid semantics of "myth" vs. "mythic" tell us about a concept that has been central to human society for millennia?

To understand how speakers of English use these terms currently, the internet is a great tool, providing as it does a snapshot of a vast linguistic community. But to get a deeper sense of how we came to speak of "myth" disparagingly, while appreciating the "mythic," one needs to dig into the layers of previous speech habits, through the history of language and philology (the art or science of interpreting and restoring texts, often in older stages of a language). A little of this goes a long way to showing that the basic roots of "myth" are grounded in story and narrative. At the same time, as some historical investigation can demonstrate, it is this very connection with the essentially social motivations for tale-telling that produces the spectrum of shades, dark and light, negative and positive, we find coloring the concept at the heart of this book – myth. We have to backtrack by two stages to appreciate the complexity of this word, looking first at its development in English and then going back almost three millennia to archaic Greece.

By common consensus, the *Oxford English Dictionary* serves as the authoritative statement of what our words mean – and have meant – as far back as documents in the language survive. The *OED* defines "myth" as "a traditional story, typically involving supernatural beings or forces, which embodies and provides an explanation, aetiology, or justification for something such as the early history of a society, a religious belief or ritual, or a natural phenomenon." We'll investigate just how well that definition fits Classical mythology a bit later in this book. But first here's a surprise: the earliest occurrence that the editors of the *OED* can find dates back only to 1830. It seems that writers in the era of Queen Victoria were the first to start spreading the use of the ancient Greek word *muthos* modified into English as "myth." Alongside its neutral meaning of "fanciful story," the negative shadings ("lie, falsehood") quickly became part of popular speech. The novelist George Eliot (aka Mary Ann Evans) in a letter of 1854 reported "Of course many silly *myths* are already afloat about me, in addition to the *truth*." Here's another surprise: the adjective made its appearance (at least in print) nearly two centuries before the noun, as far as the *OED* can tell. Theophilus Gale, a theologian, could use it to refer to something that comes from a story or a fable, in his 1669 *Court of Gentiles*, speaking of "*Mythic*, or Fabulous, Theologie, at first broached by the Poets." For some reason, the adjective never acquired the negative spin of the noun. Instead, calling something mythical meant "as in a myth" (not "as in a lie"). And by the twentieth century "mythic" had become a way of saying "awesome," "legendary," or, better yet, "fabulous" – yet another enthusiastic praise word that started out meaning "as in a story" (Latin *fabula*).

We might want to dismiss this shiftiness of "myth" within English as simply a symptom of modern speakers failing to grasp what had been central in a more stable ancient concept. As it turns out, we would be wrong. The Greeks themselves, starting in the Classical period (c. 500–300 BC) used the word *muthos* in at least three different meanings:

- word
- fiction
- purpose or thought.

What this philological excursion indicates is that, built into the notion of "myth" from a very early period, there was a basic ambiguity: is *muthos* something deeply *true* or decidedly *false*? In order to explore that question we need to push back one further stage into the history of the word, to the earliest continuous Greek texts, the epics of Homer (c. 700 BC). In the more than 27,000 lines of the *Iliad* and *Odyssey*, the noun *muthos* or verb forms derived from it occur about 350 times, providing plenty of passages for us to analyze in forming an idea of the core meaning of the concept. Through the conversation of characters or the practice of the Homeric narrator, and the situations in which the concept arises, we can get more precise indications of meaning. (This is the basic job of lexicography, to determine the semantics of a word-field – and for much of ancient Greek and Latin, the exacting work is still to be carried out.)

So what does the word that gives us "myth" mean in Homeric Greek? Three aspects of the semantic field emerge, at first sight hard to reconcile with one another.

Muthos and derivatives refer to:

- commands
- speeches of insult, invective, or abuse
- recollections and stories based on memory.

Muthos as a word

An example of the first meaning comes when Agamemnon, the commander of the Greek forces besieging Troy, rejects a plea from an aged priest on the enemy side, who has risked his life to ransom his captive daughter. The poet says that the Greek dismissed the old man with a "harsh *muthos*" and then quotes Agamemnon's threatening orders: "don't let me find you here again ... I won't return the girl ... go away so that you get off safely (*Il.*1.25–32). The priest "feared him and obeyed the *muthos*" (*Il.*1.33).

There are many commands designated *muthos*, most of which are straightforward orders. But given the tone of some speeches of command, like this speech of Agamemnon, it is easier to understand how the word might blend into the next category of meanings – abusive language. When, for example, in the great battle of the Olympians in Book 21 of the *Iliad* the war-god Ares is about to stab Athena, he addresses her with an insulting little speech (*Il.*21.393–99):

"You dog-fly, why are you causing the gods to clash with one another?" Recalling that earlier in the battle Athena had paired up with the Greek hero Diomedes to wound him, Ares goes on to vow vengeance and then makes his thrust at her, but strikes only her magical tasseled shield, the *aegis*. She in turn fells him with a boulder thrown at his head.

Here, too, there is some conceptual overlap. Just as some commanding-*muthoi* (plural of *muthos*) can be abusive, some abuse-*muthoi* can summon up a version of the past – one that puts the speaker in the best light. That rhetorical strategy is, after all, a well-known practice in trash-talking, ancient and modern: you remind the opposition of all the times that you beat them or tell them how it's now payback time for their past insults.

The third semantic area covered by the word that ultimately gives us "myth" appears to be the most promising for the eventual usage of the word. Recollections and stories built on memories can easily slip into "myths" if the past that one recalls happens to be the distant time of gods and heroes. For Menelaus, whose errant wife Helen was the immediate cause of the Trojan War, his old war-buddy Odysseus is like that: a figure out of the past. Before he was able to guess the identity of the newly arrived Telemachus, his friend's son, who has come to Sparta for news of his long-missing father, Menelaus observed that the young man wept when "recollecting about Odysseus, I spoke a *muthos* (*mutheomên*) about all the things that man endured and suffered for my sake." In other words, Menelaus calls his memories of an old heroic friend the *muthos* about the man. We can detect here the kernel that will later expand into the usage of the word *muthos* to mean recollections of long-ago heroic events. What might seem odd is that Menelaus himself, to us a figure from the world of myth, appears to be "mythologizing" his beloved companion.

Now, what are we to make of a wider semantic field in which commands, insults, and memories all interact, like circles in a Venn diagram? This turns out to be the most important, although unfamiliar, feature of the word's use, and it can lead us to understand how the concept developed over the long term. Looking at the various particular ways in which *muthos* and its derivative terms are used in Homeric poetry, one can say that the word indicates a speech, often performed in detail and in public, in which the speaker asserts responsibility and power (Agamemnon dismissing an underling,

Ares threatening his half-sister Athena). What is more, the ultimate power is control of memory. Being able to articulate "the way things were," to set the story straight the way *you* want, and to adorn it with so much detail that it is totally convincing – such is the power of a *muthos*. It is a verbal performance (a key aspect to which we'll return) that makes for an authoritative utterance. A *muthos*, in the earliest Greek narratives to which we have access, is an acting-out of authority. But that is precisely why it can be both persuasive and unstable: it is vulnerable to being contested and exposed. The concept of *muthos* teeters precariously between a truth (the way the speaker wants the story to go) and a lie (the way an addressee, who sees things differently – maybe because she is from a different region or tribe or powerful family – might perceive it). This dynamic, powered by all sorts of specific social interactions, from the very beginning of the word's history kept the concept of "myth" fluid and open to interpretation. That is part of its power and appeal. It's also why the modern word has inherited a confusing ambiguity as to what the word means.

MYTH AND COMMUNITY TRADITIONS

If myth, even in the earliest attestations of the Greek word, involves personal self-assertions, telling tales and shaping the past in a way that makes the individual speaker look authoritative, why do we *still* have such stories? Another way of asking this: why did *personal* verbal performances concerned with some past moment in time become *culturally important* goods and subsequently get passed down from the first millennium BC to us?

Clearly, what counts first is the ability to persuade a wider audience. If the circle of listeners to a mythic tale had good reasons for wanting to believe it – say, it supported a family's claim to some land, or to maintaining a status and privileges in the community – persuasion would not be difficult. A number of Greek myths must have started this way. In Athens, one aristocratic family, the Lykomidai, to which the famous fifth-century BC politician Themistocles belonged, traced its origin to a hero named Lykos (Wolf), who was reportedly a son of the mythical Athenian king, Pandion. (The king's daughters, Procne and Philomela, featured in a gory well-known myth, about which more later.) We can imagine that the clan readily passed down stories of their ancient royal origins – as, no doubt, did other kin groups with similarly blue-blooded aspirations in democratic Athens and all over the Greek world. Furthermore, the mythic tradition was probably regularly "updated" in light of the family's ongoing experiences. Thus, Lykos, in myth, was said to have been banished from Athens by his brother Aegeus (the future father of the great local hero Theseus). He fled overseas to a region (now in southwestern Turkey) that was subsequently called "Lykia" (in his honor). Themistocles, about 900 years after this mythic ancestor, fell out of favor with the Athenians, despite his key role in their battles against Persia in 480 and 479 BC, and was "ostracized" by a formal vote used to ban unpopular figures from the city for ten years. His ultimate place of exile was also in Asia Minor. Did he accidentally re-trace the journey of Lykos? Or did the story of Lykos itself become unobtrusively modified to establish a face-saving precedent for Themistocles' fate? In what seems like an anachronistic paradox, Lykos, in myth, goes to Lykia *because* Themistocles, in actuality, went there.

We can follow this tale a bit further to catch sight of another aspect of myth-making dynamics. Why was the mythic hero Lykos important in the first place? Just because the Lykomidai were successful and retrojected their genealogy back to Athenian royalty? That alone provides, as it were, only one anchor in the churning seas of political maneuvering and assertions that marked most ancient Greek life. It took another anchoring device to ensure that Lykos was a viable, prominent ancestral hero. It happened that, not far from the center of Athens, there was a park and exercise-ground called the *Lukeion*. As with every topographical feature in Greece, behind the name lay a story. This *Lukeion* was said to have been named after Lykos, son of Pandion. But at the same time, it was known as the location of a shrine dedicated to Apollo under his frequent cult-title "Lykeios" (literally "of the wolf"). Why Apollo had this byname was in turn the subject of several myths, among them the story that when he performed a year's enforced servitude to the mortal king Admetus, one of his jobs was to keep wolves away from the royal flocks. A separate site-specific tale (recorded in an ancient commentary to a speech by the great orator Demosthenes) claimed that long ago Athens once experienced a dangerous explosion of its wolf population. Apollo's oracle at Delphi told the Athenians to perform a sacrifice at this spot, and the wolves perished from its smell (though why the scent of roasting meat would kill, rather than attract, wolves, remains unclear – was it to bait them?). Whatever the reason, the merging of the hero Lykos with the god under his guise of *Lykeios* and their joint connection with the *Lukeion* cemented the importance of the hero (and his clan) in the Athenian imagination.

· As with so many Greek mythic traditions, there's more to the story that extends into the present day. This open field and its adjacent groves were also associated with Apollo in his role as the god who presides over the transition of young men to manhood (on which see Chapter 2). That was probably why a gymnasium complex developed at the site. Socrates, who frequented gathering spots for youths, spent time there. From at least the sixth century BC, the grounds were used as well for political meetings and military exercises – important institutions in the life of Athenian male citizens. The philosopher Plato (427–347 BC) established his school in a grove dedicated to the hero *Akadêmos*, on the other side of the city, which thus became known as "the Academy" (which is where we get the modern word). So when Aristotle, the pupil of Plato, was searching for a place to found his own school in the fourth century BC, another hero-grove, with convenient access to water and a stadium, made sense. He chose the *Lykeion* – giving the European languages another word for a school: "Lyceum." In the modern French educational system (thanks to a Classicizing gesture by the emperor Napoleon in 1802) the public secondary school is called *Lycée*. Excavations starting in 1996 have uncovered what archaeologists believe are the remains of Aristotle's school – possibly its library or a building for athletics. Located in an upscale city block that is bounded by a military officers' club, the War Museum, and the Athens music conservatory, it appears that the area has continued to be associated with at least some of its ancient functions.

Power-politics and propaganda campaigns made full use of mythic traditions (then as now). The "invention of tradition" served as a convenient means of connecting people with their past while shading over features that might be less useful in the present.

The rapidly evolving society of Athens in the sixth and fifth centuries BC provides a number of examples. Two in particular are worth analyzing a bit further.

Cleisthenes, son of Megacles, was a political reformer in Athens during the late sixth century BC. He is credited with making the most important practical changes that enabled true democracy to take hold on the city's political scene. To break the power of wealthy landowning families, the aristocrats who had managed Athens from time immemorial, Cleisthenes (himself an aristocrat but with the backing of the common people) reorganized the population. He assigned people of the 139 local districts ("demes") that made up the territory around Athens (the region of "Attica") to one of ten newly created tribes. Previously, people from adjacent areas (often kin to one another) had acted together, but Cleisthenes' reform meant that those of one village would be mixed in with people of a different tribe from their neighbors', and, by the same token, any one of the ten tribes would mix together people of all sorts and degrees, from diverse areas of the region – coast-dwellers with mountain-men and so forth. This brilliant move therefore ensured that a whole range of opinion and local issues would be debated whenever the new "tribe" gathered at its assembly. The tribal unit became the basis for participation in the Athenian democracy – a very new and untried phenomenon at the time. Whenever a citizen competed in local athletics contests, danced and sang in religious choruses, or fought in war, he did so as a member of his tribe.

To ease the transition while ensuring the loyalty and engagement of people in the new divisions, Cleisthenes employed myth. Each of the ten new tribes was named for a legendary Athenian king or hero. These were already familiar figures, so their newness consisted simply in their stories being redirected for a sociopolitical purpose. They included men like Cecrops, the primeval king who was said to have introduced the pre-Olympian cult of Kronos and Rhea at Athens; Aegeus, famous father of Theseus; and Hippothon, son of Poseidon (a more shadowy figure associated with Eleusis, and thus representing an Athenian claim on that once-independent community to its west). Each of the so-called "eponymous heroes" would be venerated by its tribe, by this means producing the feeling that the given set of citizens were more like an extended family group united by worship. By highlighting the myths of these long-ago figures devoted to the city-state, Cleisthenes also fostered patriotism and pride (a function that national myths still perform in the twenty-first century).

But myth was not just a tool to build democracy. Nearly half a century before Cleisthenes, another Athenian, named Peisistratus (c. 600–527 BC), used the power of mythical storytelling to cement his claim to one-man rule over the city. He traced his own ancestry, first, to the legendary Neleus, father of the Trojan War hero Nestor, who came from Pylos in the far west of the Peloponnese. (In fact, some claimed that Peisistratus secretly inserted his claim to the ancestral tie into texts of Homer's *Odyssey*, which identifies one of Nestor's sons – otherwise unknown to tradition – with exactly this name.) Then, just as Athena in the Homeric epics was well known for aiding Greek heroes like Odysseus, Achilles, and Nestor, so, too, Peisistratus lay claim to Athena's patronage, in a highly theatrical gesture.

Exiled once from power, he staged a return to Athenian territory in 556 BC by recruiting a young woman named Phya, more than six feet tall, from a rural village, dressing her as the goddess Athena (in full armor) and placing her in a chariot alongside himself. Heralds running in front of them invited the Athenians to welcome Peisistratus, "whom Athena herself honors above all men and is bringing back to her own Acropolis." And they believed! Even Herodotus, the fifth-century historian who records this incident, remarks on the crowd's gullibility – especially strange, he says, since Greeks are more clever than foreigners, and Athenians more than other Greeks. A historian of the twentieth century, however, all too aware of how political propaganda with its myths has generated extreme enthusiasm in many places, would be less surprised. Mythologizing oneself, through such assertions of continuity with the legendary past or closeness to the divine, fascinates the crowd. Then again, the Athenians, with their delight in dramatic productions of all kinds, might just have played along in admiration of the tyrant's own daring ruse, and to enjoy the show.

One should not get the impression that only Athenians manipulated traditional myth. Every community seems to have had its local heroes, who trailed behind them legends of their deeds and skirmishes (on which see Chapter 3). With so many stories floating around, there were bound to be contradictions. As we have already seen, a *muthos* is at base a question of speech and assertion. But different Greek city-states living cheek by jowl inevitably saw their historical traditions differently. This means that their own cherished *muthos* (as a national truth) would be held up against their neighbors' tale – which then

Figure 1.1 Athena, helper of heroes, in armor and wearing her snake-fringed
        aegis (with Gorgon's head), watches Heracles as he tries to steal
        Apollo's tripod from the god's Delphic oracle site. Red-figure
        amphora attributed to the Andokides painter (c. 525 BC)

became a "myth" compared to their own. A laconic sentence from
the travel writer Pausanias (second century AD) expresses neatly
what must have been the general skepticism resulting from this noisy
climate: "The Corinthian land is a portion of the Argive, and is

named after Korinthos. That Korinthos was a son of Zeus I have never known anybody say seriously except the majority of the Corinthians" (Book 2.1.1, trans. W. H. S. Jones).

Yet the traditions of communities – whether cities or families – proved useful, on the larger social stage, if employed in the right way. Indeed, diplomatic relations in the Mediterranean world many times came down to a mutual understanding between Greeks and others (e.g. people of places they wished to colonize) that the two parties were kin, related by common descent from some distant ancestor. That required investment by both sides in the veracity of myths. It is said that the indefatigable conqueror Alexander the Great, arriving among a tribal people called the Siboi, in what is now Pakistan, was able to establish friendly relations because they had been settled in their own place by the hero Heracles many centuries before, while Alexander believed that his Macedonian dynasty descended from a hero named Temenos – a son of Heracles. Nearly two centuries before Alexander, the Persian king Xerxes had tried to persuade the people of Argos not to go to war with his nation, since he was a descendant of Perses, a son of the famous Perseus, while they inhabited that hero's native place. (The Argives were impressed enough by this mythic logic that they made every effort to remain neutral.)

MYTH AND BELIEF

So, did the Athenians who lined the road to the Acropolis in 556 BC really "believe" that the tall girl riding with the ambitious war-hero-turned-politician was "really" Athena? How do we know – even about friends and family, let alone complete strangers, in the present day – what *anyone* believes? Can we safely talk about the beliefs of an entire population at some distant point in time? The very notion needs interrogation before we enter into the knotty question of whether the Greeks "believed" their myths.

Realistically, we should be speaking of a *range* of beliefs, as shown by the willingness of individuals or societies to act certain ways based on particular narratives. We are not talking about facts, so much as perceptions through the second-hand experience of being told about something. The reason that people do not usually willingly step out of third-floor windows is because they are personally aware of the fact of gravity – even if they don't have a theory about it, or a developed "belief" in its existence. They just know it operates (like sunrise, snowstorms, snake bites, or sex). But gods or demons or ghosts or angels are different. You might recognize the action of such beings when something good, bad or unexpected happens, but only because you had already been made aware that other people think such unseen powers exist. And *they* think that way because they have been told – and so on. To return to the village maiden "Athena" in the chariot of Peisistratus: the poetry of Homer had already encouraged people to imagine that a goddess could step into a chariot, take the reins, and drive with her hero into battle (as Athena is shown doing in Book 5 of the *Iliad*).

Of course, at some points in the chain of such belief in the supernatural, traditions often posit a figure – mystic, saint, or kinsman of the gods – who had direct, unmediated contact with the world beyond, whether divinities or mysterious powers. In Greek tradition, as we shall see in the next chapter, there is no single divine Revelation. On the other hand, there are moments of direct contact when a god (usually Zeus) or goddess (such as Dawn) abducts and makes love to a mortal. When these experiences result in offspring, it makes the original divine encounter instantly part of a belief system, especially (as we have already seen) when a powerful clan later traces its origins to such moments. And we cannot discount the power of poetry, which shaped for the Greeks their conception of how the gods and heroes of myth behaved. It is more than a mere literary conceit that both Homer and Hesiod speak of direct contact with the Muses, goddesses of song and the arts. Hesiod claims he met the Muses on a mountainside – we'll examine this in more detail in the next chapter. Homeric epics begin with "invocations" to the Muse to tell the stories of Achilles and Odysseus – so that the resulting lengthy narratives should be thought of as information coming directly from a timeless divine eyewitness. As the poet puts it when he asks for the Muses' help in recalling each detail of the long Catalogue of Ships (*Iliad*, Bk. 2.485–86), "You are goddesses, you are present, you know all; we, on the other hand, only hear the glorious report (*kleos*) and know nothing." The "blindness" of Homer, whether or not it was real, is an apt symbol of the murk surrounding the stories of the Trojan War, a fog of possible misinformation that only the divine Muses can cut through.

Other moments of epiphany, beyond these paradigmatic poetic contacts, can occur in dreams, or on the field of battle, according to Greek lore. This experience is not just a matter of anonymous myth but finds its way into texts and inscriptions well into the historical period, recorded (most likely) from oral testimonies close to the time of the events. Just before the battle of Marathon in September, 490 BC, the Athenians who had gathered to repel the Persian invaders sent the long-distance runner, Philippides, to ask the Spartans for aid. He covered 150 miles in two days (in vain, since the Spartans agreed to come only after the full moon, days later). On his return Philippides reported that he had seen the god Pan while running through Arcadia. The god of the wild had spoken to him, rebuking the Athenians for not paying him proper attention. The Athenians believed what Philippides said and built a sanctuary for Pan on the slope of the Acropolis, celebrating him each year with a sacrifice and a torch race. It is not impossible that Herodotus writing about this some fifty years later had access to people who had heard the runner's story first-hand. The combination of a convincing "live" account (why would the runner make it up?), with the actual Athenian success at Marathon, may well have convinced people that the divine encounter really took place, and that the god was on their side.

At the same time, as psychologists know, it does not take hallucinations to make people believe what, objectively, never took place. Memory can play tricks, and we can project our own hopes and desires onto the past. All this affects "belief." In a way, seeing what a person or group *wants* to believe is even more instructive than trying to figure out whether something really happened. One story goes that after the Greek victory at Marathon, the Athenians came to honor the legendary Theseus as a semi-divine hero especially because many of their warriors in the fight thought they saw his apparition (*phasma*) fully armed, rushing ahead in front of them against the Persians. Plutarch, who transmits this report in his *Life of Theseus* (Ch. 35) lived more than 500 years after the event. But oral traditions, it has consistently been shown, begin to lose their accuracy after 200 years have elapsed (approximately five generations). A fifth-century BC wall painting in the Painted Porch (*Stoa Poikile*), a monument in the marketplace of Athens, depicted Theseus emerging from the earth at the battle – but not leading the charge. Athena and Heracles were also in the picture, and no one was reported as saying that those figures were actually seen on the field. But it may well be that some veterans, around at the time the painting was made, attributed their completely unlikely success over the Persians to some sort of divine intervention. The "belief" visualized in the painting, in this case, is not so much a literal assertion of an actual viewing, but an effective expression of a more diffuse feeling of supernatural presence one may have got on the spot. The feeling was real, even if it indicated belief in possibilities rather than ascertainable fact.

At this point, we need to pause for a moment. It is one thing to speak of mythic narratives that were believed by some part of the population, and another to talk about belief in gods, isn't it? Aren't stories about mysterious apparitions and the deeds of famous ancestors qualitatively different from religious ideas? While we shall examine in more detail in the next chapter the lack of a boundary in Greek culture between "myth" and "religion," it is worth pointing out here a few facts about Greek practices that make such a distinction difficult. Few if any rituals or festivals of the gods were without some backstory that explained their origins. In other words, narrative was built into "religious" activity. That term has to be placed within scare quotes because *religio* is a Latin word for a very Roman concept (literally "binding back," which represents the communication between gods and humans as involving contractual and legal constraint). Greek had no equivalent word for religion, instead referring simply to *ta hiera* ("the holy things") or *ta hosia* ("things set aside for the divine"). Greek religious activity cherished no sacred book or set dogma; it had no dedicated priesthood that transmitted doctrine (priests being most often a cross between caretakers of shrines and civic officials); there was no exclusivity – one could believe in any number of gods, Greek and foreign, without being heretical. Popular poetry, built on mythic stories of gods and heroes, came to play a role somewhat like that of the Bible in Judeo-Christian belief – except one was never required to *believe* them.

THE RANGE OF TRADITION

A tradition is literally "what is handed over" (from Latin *tradere*). When we think of traditions, we imagine some group's agreement

on a tale, custom, or set of facts – maybe a family, or an intergen-
erational kin group, or village. Traditions can be purely linguistic
and highly regional (for instance, in Boston, Massachusetts, where
I grew up, the word "tonic" refers to fizzy beverages like Pepsi,
root beer or ginger ale – to the bemusement of people from regions
where these are "soda" or "pop"). Tradition can also be simple
practical habits (another Boston custom: putting out a lawn chair to
stake a claim on a street parking space laboriously excavated after a
big snowstorm). Popular traditions include festivals – like *Carnaval*
in Rio or the Mummers Parade in Philadelphia. These inspire devotion, loyalty, intensity, and passionate concern each year that the
event be done exactly in the right way. Such traditions – whether
we call them customs, rituals, or entertainments – are material for
anthropologists and folklorists, the two fields from which students
of mythology have most to learn. To put it simply, myth and religion are, in ancient Greece, complementary parts of tradition and
so tend to blend together. My example of Boston traditions might
sound completely trivial – but try telling that to a native Bostonian.
In the same way, we cannot readily, from the standpoint of our own
allegedly advanced technological culture, pluck out the trivial from
the highly serious in Greek mythico-religious tradition. At most we
can try to pin down how widespread or limited a certain feature
may have been.

A good sense of how local lore, custom, and religious belief all
merge with one another comes from reading texts like Plutarch's
Greek Questions (first–second century AD). Here the learned antiquarian collects interesting puzzles that must have been topics of
conversation at drinking parties or on the street. They might concern words: who is the *hypekkaustria* ("she who kindles the fire")
in Soli? (The priestess of Athena, who sacrifices and carries out
ceremonies to keep away evil.) Or beliefs in the power of certain people: persons credited with averting attacks of epilepsy were
known as Averters at Argos (and were thought to descend from
an ancient Argive hero). Rituals are wrapped up with wordlore
but also myth: the Argives use the word *enknisma* for the special
roasted meat made from a fire lit from the hearth of others when a
family performs a mourning sacrifice to Apollo. (Their own fire is
extinguished as being "polluted" by the death.) A clan's name on
Ithaca gets explained in terms of a myth about Telemachus the son
of Odysseus bestowing freedom on the family pig herder Eumaeus.

The taboo against a flute player entering a shrine on Tenedos is said to have arisen because one of these professionals (Molpus) long ago engineered a plot against a Trojan War era hero Tenes who was then exiled to the island. Why does the priest of Heracles on Cos wear women's clothing when he sacrifices? Well, that's a long story . . . but Plutarch will tell you.

Dozens of mythic traditions at Athens have a claim to being serious, widely believed and influential, but one especially stands out: the belief in autochthony.

"Autochthony" (from the Greek compound "earth itself" or "having the same earth") signifies the notion that a population has primeval ties to the soil in which it lives. A number of ancient peoples – the Arcadians of central Greece, the Sicani of Sicily, the Libyans – thought that they were the first humans, arising in their own place. The aristocracy of Thebes in Boeotia traced its roots to the Spartoi ("sown men"), warriors who sprang from the ground when Cadmus, the city's founder, killed a dragon and sowed its teeth. One cannot get much more literally "autochthonous." (The Spartans used a variant of the myth to explain their own name.) The inhabitants of Aegina, an island near Athens, claimed descent from ants that crawled out of the earth and were metamorphosed into people (thereafter called "Myrmidons" – from *murmêx*, "ant"). But it was the Athenians who seem to have developed the idea most thoroughly, using myth and religious rites to persuade themselves and others of its truth.

According to Athenian mythic history, their early king Erichthonius (sometimes merged with another royal figure, Erechtheus) was born from the soil on the Acropolis. The story went that once the metalworking god Hephaestus attempted to rape Athena, who fought him off. With a piece of wool she wiped off the semen that had fallen on her thigh and tossed it to the ground. Energy is never lost in Greek myth (as we shall see vividly in the next chapter). And so Earth (as goddess as well as a substance) produced a baby Erichthonius (either "very earthy" or "wool-earth") and presented it to Athena. The virgin goddess put the baby in a basket, along with snakes, entrusting this to three daughters of the ruling Athenian king (Cecrops), named Aglaurus, Pandrosus, and Hersê (all three relate to moisture and dew), with the order that they not peer inside. Of course, as with every folktale taboo, the command was disobeyed, and the girls in terror at what they saw leapt to their deaths off the

Figure 1.2 Aglaurus, Pandrosus, and Hersê, the daughters of Cecrops (mythical
first king of Athens) discover the snake-tailed baby Erichthonius in
a basket entrusted to them by Athena. Painting by Luca Giordano
(1634–1705)

Source: ART451365 Credit: © De A Picture Library/Art Resource, NY. The daughters of
Cecrops opening the basket which holds baby Erichthonius, oil on canvas, 76.5 x 133.5 cm.
Artist: Giordano, Luca (1634–1705). Location: Private Collection.

high cliffs of the Acropolis. In some versions, Erichthonius himself
is half-snake, from the waist down – an added monstrosity, but a
common motif worldwide in tales of autochthons (as snakes prefer
holes in the earth).

As with many site-centered myths, a set of rituals and beliefs
accompanied this bizarre story. A mysterious annual rite called the
Arrêphoria was tied to religious activities in the service of Athena
Polias ("of the city") carried out by a few selected Athenian girls,
aged seven to eleven. Living on the Acropolis for a year, they assisted
in the weaving of the large woolen cloak that draped the statue of
the goddess. As their time ended, the priestess of Athena one night
would give them some secret objects to convey in a box carried on
their heads through a small tunnel leading to a shrine of Aphrodite
further down the slope. The girls deposited their burden, and came
back up the hill with yet another secret package. The rite looks
like a symbolic initiatory journey, especially as it so clearly marks
out the realm of the virgin Athena as opposed to the sexualized
Aphrodite. Their transition from one space to the other (but then
back) is like a brief preview of the eventual entry into marriage and

family that every Athenian girl might be expected to undergo. Like the symbolism of Erichthonios himself – the truly autochthonous creature whose kingship somehow makes *all* Athenians "born from earth" – these few girls clearly echo Aglaurus and her mythical sisters in a part-for-whole enactment, modeling experiences and behavior for an entire group. This is an effect that *all* myths – inasmuch as they are representative tales – bring about. In addition this particular myth involved everyday civic roles as well. Aglaurus was said to be the first priestess of Athena, a civic office that continued through antiquity. At her sanctuary on the slope of the Acropolis, those Athenian males who had reached their eighteenth year and were called "ephebes" took an oath to defend Attica. Some generations before his time, according to the fifth-century historian Thucydides, aristocratic Athenians wore golden cicadas in their hair in an allusion to their autochthony (insects most conspicuously "born from the soil"). On a more strategic level, the earthborn nature of the Athenians was used by them as a rhetorical ploy. In the Persian War, the Athenians employed it to claim command, saying they "can demonstrate the longest lineage of all . . . and alone among the Greeks have never changed our place of habitation." (Herodotus. 7.161.3) Euripides has one of his self-sacrificing female characters express the same sentiment in a powerful speech from a tragedy no longer completely extant:

> We are not an immigrant people from elsewhere but born in our own land, while other cities are founded as it were through board-game moves, different ones imported from different places. But someone who settles in one city from another is like a bad peg fixed in a piece of wood: he's a citizen in name, but not in reality.
>
> (Euripides, *Erechtheus* fragment. 360, trans. Collard and Cropp)

Finally, the Athenian myth of autochthony could serve as a model for democracy – after all, if everyone came from the earth (via Erichthonios), they were all kin, all equals.

It would take us too far from the analysis of "tradition" to delve into the fascinating connections that any one myth, such as those we have sketched, can evoke in regard to a god or goddess. But it is worth pointing out once more how the folktale-like stories (say, of the three daughters of Cecrops) simultaneously shore up religious belief. Athena and Athens, of course, had been associated as far back as written records go, although it is unclear whether the city was named for the goddess or vice versa. In Athenian mythology she wins the right to be patroness of the city after a dispute with Poseidon, in which she made the winning offer, an olive tree (the sea god gave brackish water). Athena, as city protectress, must also be a warrior. She uses as weapons the *aegis* (a snake-trimmed magical goatskin – giving us the phrase "under the aegis of") and the snaky head of the Gorgon, immobilized into the center of her shield. In this role she nurtures young men (such as the ephebes). Epic poetry and heroic myths, as we have noted, support that function with constant depictions of the goddess helping heroes, whether Achilles, Odysseus, Perseus, or Jason. As goddess of craft and cunning intelligence, she also oversees the work of women: their weaving and spinning. This in turn was featured at her great annual festival, the Panathenaia, that began each new year in Athens. On the 28th day of Hekatombaion (July/August) the woolen robe which the women and young girl assistants had woven for the statue of the goddess was carted to the Acropolis unfurled on the mast of a wheeled ship.

Did every myth, then, have such deep roots in cults, festivals, rituals, and social institutions? Sometimes such connections are difficult to perceive, despite the ongoing work of modern mythologists working with all available evidence. Take, as a final example, the story of another set of young Athenian women mentioned in passing earlier, the daughters of Pandion (a son of Erichthonius), named Procne and Philomela.

Procne was given in marriage to Tereus of Thrace (for Athenians, a wild northern region) because he helped her father in a local war. But he became infatuated with her sister, raped her, and cut out her tongue to prevent word getting out. Philomela's only recourse was to weave the story of her sufferings into a robe, which she sent to Procne. Reunited with her sister, Procne than killed Itys, her own son by Tereus, cooking and serving the dismembered body to her husband. Tereus chased both sisters with a double axe, but on the point of being murdered, they were turned into birds. Procne, constantly lamenting her son, became a nightingale, while Philomela, who could only twitter, changed into a swallow. Tereus became a woodpecker-like bird called *epops*.

Figure 1.3 Before the avian metamorphosis: Procne presents her husband
       Tereus with the head of their son Itys (upon whose body he has just
       unknowingly dined), as her sister Philomela looks on. Painting by
       Peter Paul Rubens, c. 1635

Source: ART215264 Photo Credit: Erich Lessing/Art Resource, NY. The banquet of
Tereus: Philomena and Procne present Tereus the decapitated head of his son Itys, whose
flesh he has eaten. Painted for the "Torre de La Parada." Location: Museo del Prado,
Madrid, Spain.

There are a few indications that the myth had something to do with
rituals. For instance, the detail that Itys was roasted as well as boiled
seems to be related to a taboo on such cooking by the sixth-century
BC Orphics, followers of doctrines attributed to the mythical singer
Orpheus. The sisters are described as frenzied "Bacchants," involved
in worshiping Dionysos (whose rites, in turn, were connected with
Orphism). And there is the strange detail that at Megara west of
Athens the grave of Tereus was shown, at which every year a sacrifice was made with gravel being thrown rather than barley groats – a
symbolic stoning of the evil king. Yet, even if the myth is somehow
related to old beliefs about guilt or the origins of bird species, the
most important function of the story was undoubtedly its expression of universally powerful feelings – love and lust, jealousy and

revenge, despair and release. Most of the details we possess probably derive from a play by the tragedian Sophocles (produced sometime before 414 BC) that survives only in quotations. It is clear that he saw in the myth an opportunity to win the dramatic contest by rousing the emotions of his audience with a vivid story of murder, marriage and metamorphosis – perhaps with a hint of Athenian animus against Thrace, a "barbarian" region about which the city was decidedly ambivalent. In any event, with the Tereus complex we seem to hover at the opposite end of the spectrum of tradition, with an exotic, but less politically and socially embedded myth.

REJECTING MYTH

The extreme violence of Greek myth, its frank sexuality, and often amoral characters did not go unnoticed even in antiquity. Even as myths were being passed down by poets and dramatized by Athenian playwrights, various ways of interpreting traditional tales were developed that sought to overwrite this content in favor of more ethically oriented messages abut gods and heroes. In this section and the next two, we shall look briefly at some strategies for saving myth from itself – interpretive moves that can still be found in modern treatments.

Xenophanes was a poet and philosopher of the sixth century BC, the first of the so-called "Pre-Socratics." A native of Ionia (now the coast of western Turkey), he eventually moved to a Greek settlement in Sicily. As with other early writers, no continuous work of his survives; instead, we have quotations and paraphrases and allusions. Among the most striking are several that seem to imagine a world moved by a single god, who remains unknowable. Xenophanes rejects the traditional Greek method of making divinities look like humans (anthropomorphism): "if oxen and horses or lions had hands, and could paint with their hands, and produce works of art as men do, horses would paint the forms of the gods like horses, and oxen like oxen" (this and following translations are by J. Burnet). Even humans cannot agree on their depictions, as it is just culturally relative: "The Ethiopians make their gods black and snub-nosed; the Thracians say theirs have blue eyes and red hair." Phenomena that were traditionally associated with signs from the gods – St Elmo's Fire and the rainbow – were debunked by Xenophanes as purely atmospheric, not (respectively) the presence of Castor and Pollux on a ship's forestay or the goddess Iris. Given this tendency to demythologize, it was not surprising that the philosopher found fault with traditional poets and their immoral divinities: "Homer and Hesiod have ascribed to the gods all things that are a shame and a disgrace among mortals, stealing and adulteries and deceiving one another." Then again, there may have been professional jealousy: at least one ancient source identified Xenophanes himself as a "rhapsode," an itinerant performer of epic-style poetry. Perhaps his objections to the others were also a way of advertising his own art.

Another critic of Homer was Heraclitus of Ephesus (c. 500 BC), also from Ionia, the center of the Greek "enlightenment" in the sixth century BC. An enigmatic thinker and coiner of paradoxical aphorisms (like "expect the unexpected" or "the way up and the way down are one and the same"), he was blunt in advising that Homer should be "thrown out of the [poetic] contests and beaten with a rod." Apparently, Heraclitus objected to the poetic handling of myths. It could also be that he found fault with a poem like the *Odyssey* when it came to its description of the underworld as a dank, hopeless place, for he himself asserted, "There await men when they die such things as they look not for nor dream of." Like Xenophanes, he seems to have had a theory that was essentially monotheistic, opposed to the multiplicity of gods found in poetry and myth: "The wise is one only," said Heraclitus. "It is unwilling and willing to be called by the name of Zeus." In contrast to the transgressive gods of Homer and Hesiod, Heraclitus imagined a strict adherence to rule, even by the cosmos, personified as gods: "The sun will not overstep his measures; if he does, the Erinyes [Furies], the handmaids of Justice will find him out." The all-too-human failings of the poet Homer, he who supposedly was in touch with the Muses, made him something of a figure of fun for the philosopher: "Men are deceived in their knowledge of things that are manifest, even as Homer was who was the wisest of all the Greeks. For he was even deceived by boys killing lice when they said to him: 'What we have seen and grasped, these we leave behind; whereas what we have not seen and grasped, these we carry away'." The statement alludes to a tradition about Homer's death on the island Ios, in despair at being unable to solve the children's riddle about their own activity (delousing).

The most famous philosopher to reject Homer was, of course, Plato. He did so on a number of grounds. First, the rhapsodes who swarmed through Greece competing in recitals of the *Iliad* and *Odyssey* may have known how to perform, and even explain the surface meanings of Homeric poetry, but they could not claim real knowledge, Plato believed. Theirs was a sort of divinely inspired madness beyond their control. Plato has Socrates, in the dialogue *Ion*, compare the relationship of Muse to poet to rhapsodic reciter (and finally audience) as being like a series of magnetic rings, each clinging to the one above it. In other words, poetry is not logical, so its myths cannot be the final, reasoned account of reality. A second objection also centers on the medium through which Homeric poetry – again the central repository of myths – was diffused. We may read texts of the epics, but most Greeks *heard* them as orally recited, even acted out. Ion, the rhapsode interrogated by Socrates, for example, talks about his histrionic ability for making an audience of several thousands cry. To Plato, this vivid enactment presents a real danger to the minds of young listeners. In an argument that will be echoed millennia later by critics of television, he dwells on the hazards of imitation, when a viewer and hearer of Homer (or other misdirected poetry) places himself in the role of a fictional character. Clearly, the imitation or *mimesis* is more threatening when experienced live, as in rhapsodic performance and theater, rather than simply read. Plato has in mind what happens to a young man when he takes on the voice of various characters. It is as if there is no way to filter what comes at you, as if playing the role of a person who suffers or laments makes you experience those feelings. But, as the Platonic Socrates insists, such psychic disturbances are deeply deleterious for the soul. Finally, wrapped up with the dangers of *mimesis* are the falsities that the poetry of Homer and Hesiod present: gods who are violent, deceptive in speech, changeable in appearance and mood, in short all that *his* idea of god (and the mystical Platonic "Ideas" themselves) are not. Poetry should not make Death appear to be an evil. It should make you courageous, unafraid to die.

As is often remarked, Plato in his *Republic* and other dialogues replaced the myths of Homer and Hesiod, which he would exile form the ideal city-state, with another set of myths of his own devising. Most striking is the elaborate story of Er at the end of the *Republic* (Book 10.614–10.621). Having tirelessly worked over the question of why one should want to be moral, the book-length dialogue ends with an eschatological motivation, in the form of a tale once heard. The mortal warrior Er had a near-death experience after being severely wounded on a battlefield. His account of the judgment of spirits after death goes into meticulous detail about the circulation of souls to a heaven-like upper realm or to a subterranean place of punishment, depending on their moral status while in the flesh. The souls travel finally to a rainbow-colored pillar of light where Necessity, the Sirens, and the Fates are installed. Tokens are handed out and the souls, by number, choose new lives for reincarnation. This is the moment for the philosophically trained discrimination learned in one's former life, so that a person will choose the new life that will make for true happiness. Er recounts the life-choices of ancient heroes, including Odysseus, weary with a king's life, who chose a future as the most obscure and ordinary of citizens. In sum, Plato's Socrates, who began with a promise not to tell the sort of story Odysseus tells in epic, ends up giving us an alternative to the Homeric *Odyssey*.

RATIONALIZING MYTH

Another ancient strategy for saving the vast mythic tradition was to seek the truth hidden in apparently immoral or disturbing stories from the past. This approach enabled interpreters to keep many of the juicy details of the original stories, while explaining their "true" underlying significance. Hecataeus of Miletus (yet another Ionian) in the later sixth century BC had the scientific spirit of his age. His book, the *Genealogies* (also called the *History of the Heroes*), begins "Hecataeus of Miletus made the follow declaration: I write down what appears true to me. For the tales (*logoi*) of the Greeks are many and ridiculous." His solution was to establish a chronology into which he could fit the many disparate stories as though they were pieces of one large historical narrative. The later historian Herodotus, while greatly influenced by him, was keen to point out his slips. He reports that Hecataeus himself could trace his personal genealogy back sixteen generations to a god (via Heracles) – but this did not impress the

Egyptian priests whom both Hecataeus and, later on, Herodotus, encountered in Egypt, with their records older by thousands of years. The efforts of Hecataeus to rationalize myths seem to have further involved stripping the old stories of any supernatural elements, while holding onto the basic plot-lines. For instance, he revised the myth about Heracles' fetching Kerberos the watchdog from an entrance to the underworld near Tainaron, a cape on the extreme south of the Peloponnese. It was not a three-headed dog, declared Hecataeus, but a venomous snake called the "hound of Hades" that Heracles brought back. Such meticulous rationalizing seems not to have squelched his urge to relay other tales that we might find implausible, like that about a son of Deucalion (survivor of the Great Flood) whose dog gave birth to a root that grew into a grape-covered vine.

Rationalizing away the scandalous or intractable elements of myth was part of the toolkit of the sophists, itinerant experts of the fifth century BC, who professed to teach anything from rhetoric to household management, for a suitable fee. Some of the more famous were Gorgias, Protagoras, and Hippias (known to us as interlocutors of Socrates in Plato's dialogues). Another sophist, Prodicus from the island Keos, gave a reasoned account of the origin of religion itself (and thus of myth), asserting among other points that "things that have become beneficial for mankind are considered deities, such as Demeter and Dionysos" – in other words, elements (Poseidon as water, Hephaestus as fire) and products of the earth (bread and wine) had been made into gods by appreciative humans. Euripides and Thucydides were said to be pupils of Prodicus, a suggestion that fits with their own rationalizing of mythic traditions in later fifth-century drama and history, respectively.

Less likely is the information that Socrates, also, was taught by this Prodicus. Although he was clearly aware of rationalizing explanations, he saw his intellectual task as more serious. In the *Phaedrus* by Plato, we see Socrates conversing with the young man for whom the dialogue is named, as they walk near the stream Ilissos in Athens. Wasn't it near here that Boreas carried off Oreithyia (a legendary king's daughter) asks Phaedrus? Do you believe the mythic account (*muthologêma*)? To which Socrates replies, in a perfect summary of his ethical ideal:

If I disbelieved, as the wise men do, I should not be extraor
might give a rational explanation, that a blast of Boreas, th
pushed her off the neighboring rocks as she was playing wi'
and that when she had died in this manner she was saic
carried off by Boreas. But I, Phaedrus, think such explanations a.. ..,
pretty in general, but are the inventions of a very clever and laborious
and not altogether enviable man, for no other reason than because after
this he must explain the forms of the Centaurs, and then that of the
Chimaera, and there presses in upon him a whole crowd of such creatures, Gorgons and Pegasuses, and multitudes of strange, inconceivable,
portentous natures. If anyone disbelieves in these, and with a rustic sort
of wisdom, undertakes to explain each in accordance with probability, he
will need a great deal of leisure. But I have no leisure for them at all; and
the reason, my friend, is this: I am not yet able, as the Delphic inscription
has it, to know myself.

(Phaedrus 229 c–e, trans. H.N. Fowler)

Probably the most influential rationalizer of myths from antiquity
was Euhemerus, who wrote in the Hellenistic period, a generation
after the death of Alexander the Great. His lost travel novel is one
of those texts that Classicists yearn to have whole. In it, according
to the meager information we possess, Euhemerus told of a voyage
to an island in the Indian Ocean called "Panchaea." There he saw a
monumental golden column on which were written all the deeds
that Ouranos, Kronos, and Zeus had accomplished. In traditional
Greek mythology, these were divinities (whom we'll examine in
the next chapter). According to the (imaginary) inscription, however (erected by Zeus himself), these three had been mortal kings
over their distant territory, later commemorated and raised to
godhood by their own people. It is not coincidental that similar
customs actually were common in the eastern lands that Alexander
had recently conquered. Alexander himself had been deified by his
successor Ptolemy I. "Euhemerism" as it came to be called did not
obliterate myths, but made them, once again, a form of historical
reminiscence. Its real success as an explanatory theory came centuries later, however, when Christian writers, such as Lactantius
(AD 240–320) used it to advance the idea of one God, the other
pagan divinities being clearly – as one pagan had discovered – just
jumped-up mortals.

ALLEGORIZING MYTH

Ancient thinkers began interpreting myth in the same time periods that new versions were being produced: we are not dealing with a sudden shift in sensibility or belief, from "mythos" to "logos" (rational account), as intellectual historians have too often characterized it. Because the prestige and influence of Homeric poetry loomed so large, the *Iliad* and *Odyssey* were prime targets for explanation. After all, these might pose a risk to the tender minds of young people who could hear them being recited each day in the marketplace, and who were taught how to read and write using the poems of Homer. One important brand of interpretation took the form of "allegory" (literally, "speaking in other terms"). It centered especially on myth as a way of talking about the physical world. Theagenes of Rhegium in southern Italy was the first, it appears, to use this when he interpreted the battle of gods in Books 20–21 of the *Iliad* as a clash between elements – dry vs. wet, hot vs. cold, and so forth. "Hera" is really air (the words sound somewhat alike in Greek), while "Apollo" (or Hephaestus the metal worker) is fire, "Poseidon" equals water and "Artemis" is the moon. Another related form of allegory turned the gods into symbolic figures for capacities and emotions: Athena represents intelligence, Aphrodite desire, Hermes speech. Using this method one can whitewash the otherwise improper spectacle of brawling divinities.

This early tendency towards allegorizing was confirmed by the discovery in January 1962 of a charred papyrus roll in a tomb at Derveni in northern Greece. Not fully published until 2006, it contains a commentary on a hexameter poem about the birth of the gods ("a theogony") attributed to the mythical figure Orpheus. The scroll itself dates from the lifetime of Alexander the Great (356–323 BC) but the text it contains was probably composed at least a century earlier. In the commentary both Zeus and Oceanus are interpreted as air, while Hera, Rhea, and Demeter are all said to be names for earth, and Olympus is not a mountain where the gods live but Time itself. Whether or not only a small minority of initiates (perhaps including the inhabitant of the tomb) were being taught such things, the approach of the Derveni papyrus does seem to fit with more general opinions holding that poetry about the gods was not about the surface plot – it contained depths and enigmas beyond superficial reading.

In the view of later educators, these less obvious meanings of Homer, Hesiod, and other myth-permeated works could be turned into moral lessons, even without the elaborate semi-mystical exegesis of the physical allegorists. Plutarch (second century AD) in a short treatise *How the Young Man Should Study Poetry* makes the distinction while discussing a risqué episode of adulterous sex between Ares and Aphrodite, in a song heard by Odysseus in the palace of Alcinous (*Odyssey* Book 8):

> By forcibly distorting these stories through what used to be termed "deeper meanings," but are nowadays called "allegorical interpretations," some persons say that the Sun is represented as giving information about Aphrodite in the arms of Ares, because the conjunction of the planet Mars with Venus portends births conceived in adultery, and when the sun returns in his course and discovers these, they cannot be kept secret.

But, says Plutarch in opposition, the context itself in which the song is performed – at an effete court of an unheroic, spoiled king – holds the key:

> In the account of Aphrodite, he [Homer] teaches those who will pay attention that vulgar music, coarse songs, and stories treating of vile themes, create licentious characters, unmanly lives, and men that love luxury, soft living, intimacy with women, and "Changes of clothes, warm baths, and the genial bed of enjoyment."
>
> (Plutarch, *Moralia* 20A)

Even though the physical allegories continued to attract attention through the Middle Ages and Renaissance, it is Plutarch's more nuanced style of moral interpretation, seeing myth as related to ethical self-development, that prevailed in the twentieth century. It flourishes still in new guises – primarily, in psychological interpretation of ancient tales.

HOW WE GET MYTH

Two important facts have to be borne in mind about the stories we read nowadays as Greek "myths." First, as we have just seen, they have already been handled and combed through by centuries of interpreters.

This means that the versions we read may well have been cleaned up, revised to fit someone's view of propriety, tailored to a recipient or an occasion, burnished to uphold a city's self-image – in short, subjected to all sorts of hidden agendas which we can no longer detect. The second principle goes along with the first: there is no such thing as monolithic Greek myth. There are versions – sometimes dozens of them – of just about every tale. We might construct our own smoothly continuous narratives by stringing together the elements that seem to be common to many versions, or by silently omitting bits that do not fit a pattern. But we can never be sure that such a narrative would interest an ancient listener, much less gain her assent.

To appreciate fully the variety of our sources, it will help to sketch (below) the range of literature and other materials in which they are represented. But first, it is worthwhile digging a little more deeply into the actual medium that gives us our earliest continuous versions of Greek tales, the poems attributed to Homer and Hesiod (both c. 700 BC). As will emerge, knowing the medium is crucial for appreciating the kind of message it envelops.

Only within the past century has the technique of making epic-style Greek verse become better understood. In brief, it has been found that poetry like Homer's is made up of hundreds of ready-made, flexible formulae that can be combined easily, in live performance, to produce any number of verses, episodes, and compositions. Specialists had long known that the mixture of dialect forms, neologisms, and archaisms in the language of Homeric poetry was the result of metrical demands. Poets needed words of the right shape to fit their lines, which consisted of six "hexameter" feet (each comprising one long syllable followed by two shorts). Even such minor items as pronouns in each grammatical case ("to me," "for me," etc.) turn out to have multiple forms, each with a different metrical shape. (In the same way nineteenth-century poets used the English dialect alternatives *o'er* and *e'er* vs. the two-syllable *over* and *ever* when they needed single syllables for the meter.) But the demonstration that entire phrases in Homer and Hesiod follow such principles of convenience only emerged in the 1920s thanks to the work of a Californian, Milman Parry. After listing all the stock phrases in Homer – the well-known system of adjectives applied to the important personages of the poems, such as "swift-footed Achilles" and "Odysseus of much cunning" – Parry proved that for each and every major heroic and divine figure in Homer there existed one (and almost always *only* one) epithet for each grammatical case (accusative, genitive, etc.). His larger conclusion was that Homeric poetry represents a multi-generational art form. It was the result of a long-term evolution, with contributions by many poets over generations: no one poet would have been able to devise such an extensive and economical system of phrases. In addition, Parry surmised that this poetic system was most likely created for the rapid composition of verse and passed down as part of a popular art form, from older to younger poets. In a second stage of his research, he and his younger collaborator Albert Lord confirmed through field-work in the former Yugoslavia that exactly such techniques were employed by illiterate poets who composed from scratch, during the course of performance, long oral poems about national heroes of the past, no two of which were ever exactly the same.

The essential findings of Parry and Lord when applied to Greek myth are two. First, myths were passed down by poems now known to have been the result of long-term oral productions – which means we cannot say for sure that any one poet (Homer, Hesiod, or other) is responsible for the tale we get, in every detail. We know that some Greek formulae must date back, on linguistic criteria, to almost the time of the Trojan War itself (if not earlier). Just as the medium was traditional, so the storylines and characters were inherited. Second, and in some ways in contrast to the first finding: because the medium was so flexible, a technique for rapid composition-in-performance that did *not* require painstaking memorization of an entire poem, the composers were freed to innovate. That is to say, a version of the *Odyssey* composed one night in 700 BC in Sparta might be completely different from another version sung in a different location a year later. Extensive studies of contemporary oral traditions from all over the world, carried out during the last fifty years, can demonstrate that poets vary their tales to fit their audiences, sometimes radically. Myths – the backbone of these oral poems – thus shift and change just as easily.

So far we have a paradox – myths can be incredibly old but come in versions that were devised, so to speak, just yesterday. In fact, if we look closely at the *Iliad* and the *Odyssey*, we find myth-makers in the person of heroic speakers giving just such new spins to old tales. Achilles, for instance, at the end of the *Iliad* tells his enemy Priam the story of Niobe, a grief-stricken legendary mother whose children were slain by the gods (*Il*.24.601–19). He does so in order to make the point that even in deep grief one should still bear up, eat, and accept the gods' will. Ironically, Priam's own son has just been slain by Achilles, and the Greek hero himself will soon die. No other version of the Niobe tale known to us is quite like this one. Clearly, this "myth" and many other tales of the past narrated by characters in the epics, from the story of Meleager and his wife Cleopatra (*Iliad*, Book 9), to Nestor's autobiographical tales of youthful exploits (*Iliad*, Book 11), are shaped by their immediate rhetorical situation, as men or women try to persuade one another by citing exemplary narratives. We must assume that the epics capture something authentic about the actual deployment of myths by Greeks, in everyday discourse.

The range of variation offered by myths would most likely have depended on the occasions for telling. If oral poets, composing in performance, competed against one another in front of large crowds – as seems to have happened with the poetry of Homer and Hesiod – there may have been motivations to introduce shocking new details. We have traces of some: for instance, the myth (attributed to the sixth-century poet Steischorus) that Helen never went to Troy. Instead the whole war that followed her abduction by Paris from Greece was fought over a phantom, which the gods had substituted for the real woman, who was safely tucked away in Egypt while the ten-year siege wore on. (Euripides in the later fifth century made a semi-comic drama out of this alternative version.) On one hand, myths that accompanied a festival of Theseus each year must have been widely variable: by telling stories, people imitated mothers of the legendary Athenian youths sent to the Minotaur's den in Crete, who had originally spun out tales to comfort their doomed children. On the other hand, at ritual events myths might be repeated in fairly stylized and consistent form. The clan of the Lycomidai (mentioned above) knew short hymns by Orpheus and chanted them over the mysteries. In liturgical use, where there is no need to entice or entertain an immediate audience with novelties, variation shrinks.

Two concluding passages are useful for showing that the writers who conveyed Greek myths were perfectly aware of this malleability. In his most famous work, the fifth-century poet Pindar, who undertook commissions to celebrate victors in the athletics contests, recalls the story of Pelops, associated with the founding of the

Olympic games. The traditional tale was that this hero had been killed and cooked by his father, Tantalus, then served up to test some unsuspecting gods. Only Demeter, distracted with grief for her missing daughter Persephone, ate her portion (a shoulder), the other gods having caught on to the horrible trick. (Restored to life, Pelops therefore had to receive an ivory replacement for this part of his body.) Not true, says Pindar: common talk among people goes far beyond a reasonable account (*logos*) and leads to stories (*muthoi*) adorned with lies. He offers a less blameworthy version:

> Son of Tantalus, of you I shall say, contrary to my predecessors,
>
> that when your father invited the gods
>
> to his most orderly feast and to his friendly Sipylos,
>
> giving them a banquet in return for theirs,
>
> then it was that the Lord of the Splendid Trident seized you,
>
> his mind overcome by desire, and with golden steeds
>
> conveyed you to the highest home of widely honored Zeus.
>
> (Trans. W. Race)

After this honor of being chosen as Poseidon's lover, however, Pelops is kicked back to earth because his father Tantalus dared to steal nectar and ambrosia from the gods and give them to his mortal drinking-buddies. Tantalus, in addition, receives his well-known punishment in the underworld for the crime, unable to reach the shifting fruit above his head or water at his feet (thus "tantalized"). Pindar goes on to explain his reluctance to accept the common myth while theorizing about how gossip creates tales: it was an envious neighbor who made up the story of Pelops being boiled in a pot, when he had actually disappeared onto Olympus. "But for my part, I cannot call any of the blessed gods a glutton – I stand back: impoverishment is often the lot of slanderers" (*Olympian.* 11.24–59).

Pindar's upright ethical stance thus moves halfway toward the moral allegorizing practiced by later interpreters. Believing the gods to be pure and just, he cannot stomach the story that even one of them had been a cannibal (unintentionally, at that). For Hesiod, however, the Greek poet and myth-teller thought to be active about 200 years before Pindar, eating one's children was simply what gods did. Without raising doubts he tells the story of Kronos devouring his offspring. Of course, that was an event of the bad old days before Zeus came to power (as will be detailed in the next chapter). Hesiod plants a small seed of doubt elsewhere in his *Theogony*, the composition that related the rise of Zeus. Meeting the Muses on his local mountain slope, Hesiod receives from them the gift of poetic song. But as they initiate him, the goddesses utter three perplexing lines, part insult, part riddle:

> Field-dwelling shepherds, ignoble disgraces, mere bellies:
>
> we know how to say many false things similar to genuine ones,
>
> but we know, when we wish, how to proclaim true things [*alêthea*].
>
> (Trans. G. Most)

In the Greek, "true things" is literally "what is not forgotten." Telling the truth, therefore, is an entirely appropriate job for the Muses, whose mother was Memory itself (*Mnêmosynê*). And the role of memory in a culture only recently discovering literacy cannot be overstated. Yet neither these lines of verse nor the rest of Hesiod's poem positively asserts that what the Muses said, at the moment they gave Hesiod his life's profession, is one or the other sort of speech. Are they telling the truth or uttering lies that are *like* it – fictions with an attractive verisimilitude – in a word, myths? One could not ask for a more concise summation of the double-edged fascination that myth produces to this day.

THE SOURCES: A BRIEF CHRONOLOGICAL LIST

This book can only touch on a few of the stories, and only briefly. The quickest way to find full versions (usually cobbled together) is through the handbooks mentioned in the Further Reading. But the most authentic way is to read the Greek and Latin texts, preferably in chronological order (and of course, best of all, in the original languages). Here are the major authors concerned with myth (although it is rare that any Greek or Latin writer fails to mention at least one such story). For almost all, there are a number of English translations easily available. The Loeb Classical Library has reliable versions in bilingual editions. (Unless otherwise identified, translations in this volume are from the Loebs.)

- Homer: *Iliad* and *Odyssey* (c. 700 BC). The last year of the Trojan War, with flashbacks to earlier events; the long voyage home of one hero.
- Hesiod: The *Theogony*. Events from the beginning of the world through the marriages of Zeus. Additional details about Pandora, the Five Ages provided by the same poet's *Works and Days*. The fragmentary *Catalogue of Women* lists love affairs between mortals and gods.
- *Homeric Hymns* (seventh–sixth centuries BC). Entertaining narratives in epic style, rather than liturgical hymns praising the Greek gods. The five longest, to Demeter, Apollo, Hermes, Aphrodite, and Dionysos, are the earliest continuous stories about those gods.
- Epic Cycle (various poets; fragments only). Poems that filled in the backstory to the Trojan saga as well as its aftermath; also tales about Heracles, the city of Corinth, and other matters.
- Pindar: *Odes* (518–438 BC). He composed many lyric pieces for singing and dancing choruses, but the *Odes* for athletes are best known and are full of allusions to myths, often highly condensed.
- Athenian tragedians. Aeschylus (c. 525–456 BC), Sophocles (c. 496–406 BC), and Euripides (c. 485–406 BC). A total of thirty-two plays survive intact, from the ninety or so each dramatist wrote. Quotations, titles, or plot summaries of others survive. The dramatists seem to have used the Epic Cycle more than the Homeric versions.
- Herodotus (c. 484–420 BC). His nine-book *Histories* about the war between Greeks and Persians embeds many myths and legends, Greek and foreign.
- Callimachus (third century BC). A scholar-poet working in Alexandria, Egypt; wrote six hymns in Homeric style, preserving stories about Zeus, Artemis, Apollo, Athena, Demeter and the sacred island Delos. His fragmentary *Aitia* ("Causes") contained many origin tales.
- Apollonius of Rhodes (third century BC). Another Alexandrian, wrote the epic *Argonautica* about Jason and the Golden Fleece.
- "Apollodorus" (first/second century AD?). The *Library* that goes under his name summarizes hundreds of myths from other sources, many of which did not otherwise survive.
- Plutarch (c. AD 50–120). Greek antiquarian and essayist, author of twenty-three "parallel lives" of famous Greeks and Romans, including mythic (to us) figures like Theseus.

- Pausanias (mid-second century AD). Greek traveller whose *Description of Greece* transmits myths connected with shrines and sanctuaries he visited.
- Vergil (70–19 BC). Poet, whose touching Latin epic, the *Aeneid*, drew on Homer, tragedy, and Alexandrian literature to tell of the Trojan who was the ultimate ancestor of the Romans.
- Ovid (43 BC–AD 17). Prolific Roman poet, his fifteen-book *Metamorphoses* focused on myths involving transformations of people to birds, trees, spiders, etc. Most influential reworking of myths in all Western literature.
- Artistic sources. Sculpture on temples (e.g. the Parthenon), frescoes, and, most of all, paintings on Greek vases (of which more than 100,000 survive) often preserve depictions of myth, sometimes of versions known from no other source.

FURTHER READING

Several reliable handbooks offer condensed versions of Classical myths, with varying levels of annotation. The most detailed is Timothy Gantz, *Early Greek Myth: A Guide to Literary and Artistic Sources* (Baltimore: Johns Hopkins University Press, 1993). Robin Hard has updated the useful older work by H. J. Rose in *The Routledge Handbook of Greek Mythology* (London: Routledge, 2003). Less detailed but bountifully illustrated is the student textbook by Mark Morford, Robert Lenardon and Michael Sham, *Classical Mythology* (10th edn, New York: Oxford University Press, 2013). An equivalent text by Barry Powell, *Classical Myth* (8th edn, Boston: Pearson, 2015) offers much of the same material but with sharper authorial opinions. The richest selection of primary texts can be found in *Anthology of Classical Myth: Primary Sources in Translation*, edited by Stephen Trzaskoma, R. Scott Smith, and Stephen Brunet (Indianapolis: Hackett Publishing, 2004). My *Myths of the Ancient Greeks* (New York: Penguin/NAL, 2003) puts together the major stories in a running narrative with novelistic touches.

For accurate and handy reference, see *The Oxford Dictionary of Classical Myth and Religion*, edited by Emily Kearns and Simon Price (Oxford: Oxford University Press, 2003). A fine introduction to the interpretive and historical contexts (also beautifully illustrated) is Richard Buxton, *The Complete World of Greek Mythology* (London: Thames & Hudson, 2011). The essays in *The Cambridge*

Companion to Greek Mythology, edited by Roger Woodard (New York: Cambridge University Press, 2007) are excellent guides to all aspects of mythology. Each of these books contains extensive suggestions for further reading.

The problem of what "myth" means, in ancient as well as modern culture, has been addressed most clearly by two specialists, Fritz Graf, *Greek Mythology: An Introduction*, trans. Thomas Marier (Baltimore: Johns Hopkins University Press, 1993) and Marcel Detienne, *The Creation of Greek Mythology*, trans. Margaret Cook (Chicago: University of Chicago Press, 1986) with interestingly different results. My study, *The Language of Heroes: Speech and Performance in the Iliad* (Ithaca: Cornell University Press, 1989) investigates the meaning of *muthos* in Homeric poetry.

Many recent works focus on myth in Athenian society and politics. Good starting points are Robert Parker, *Polytheism and Society at Athens* (Oxford: Oxford University Press, 2005); Alan Shapiro, *Art and Cult under the Tyrants in Athens* (Darmstadt: von Zabern, 1989); William Tyrrell and Frieda Brown, *Athenian Myths and Institutions: Words in Action* (New York: Oxford University Press, 1991), and Jean-Pierre Vernant, *Myth and Society in Ancient Greece*, trans. Janet Lloyd (Atlantic Highlands: Humanities Press, 1980). Especially good concerning autochthony and related notions is Nicole Loraux, *The Children of Athena: Athenian Ideas about Citizenship and the Division between the Sexes*, trans. Caroline Levine (Princeton: Princeton University Press, 1994). On cults of Athena in the city, see Jenifer Neils (ed.), *Worshipping Athena: Panathenaia and Parthenon* (Madison: University of Wisconsin Press, 1996). For the deeper roots of the Procne and Philomela myth, see Walter Burkert, *Homo Necans*, trans. Peter Bing (Berkeley: University of California Press, 1983).

Other employments of myth are well surveyed in Ken Dowden, *The Uses of Greek Mythology* (London: Routledge, 1992). On its uses in diplomacy, see Christopher P. Jones, *Kinship Diplomacy in the Ancient World* (Cambridge, MA: Harvard University Press, 1999). And for the toughest overall question, see Paul Veyne, *Did the Greeks Believe in Their Myths?*, trans. P. Wissing (Chicago: University of Chicago Press, 1988). Related to the question of beliefs is the alleged shift to rational thought, on which see the essays in *From Myth to Reason?*, ed. Richard Buxton (Oxford: Oxford University Press, 1999).

No single work in English tries to cover all ancient methods of myth interpretation, but see for particular modes: *Metaphor,*

Allegory, and the Classical Tradition: Ancient Thought and Modern Revisions, ed. G. R. Boys-Stones (Oxford: Oxford University Press, 2003); Greta Hawes, *Rationalizing Myth in Antiquity* (Oxford: Oxford University Press, 2014); Robert Lamberton, *Homer the Theologian* (Berkeley: University of California Press, 1986); and a key essay by Andrew Ford, "Performing Interpretation: Early Allegorical Exegesis of Homer," in Margaret Beissinger, Jane Tylus, and Susanne Wofford (eds.), *Epic Traditions in the Contemporary World: The Poetics of Community* (Berkeley: University of California Press, 1999). On the allegorizing Derveni papyrus, see K. Tsantsanoglou, G. M. Parassoglou, and T. Kouremenos (eds.), *The Derveni Papyrus* (Florence: Olschki Editore, 2006) as well as Gábor Betegh, *The Derveni Papyrus: Cosmology, Theology and Interpretation* (Cambridge: Cambridge University Press, 2004).

The delicate relationship between myth and literature requires sophisticated methods of reading. Outstanding guides are Gregory Nagy, *Pindar's Homer: The Lyric Possession of an Epic Past* (Baltimore: Johns Hopkins University Press, 1990) and Lowell Edmunds, *Myth in Homer: A Handbook*, (2nd edn, Highland Park, NJ: 1993). For the interplay of folktale, myth, and literary treatments, see William F. Hansen, *Ariadne's Thread: A Guide to International Tales Found in Classical Literature* (Ithaca: Cornell University Press, 2002). On the oral-formulaic technique and its implications, see Albert B. Lord, *The Singer of Tales* (2nd edn [original 1960], with introduction by S. Mitchell and G. Nagy) (Cambridge, MA: Harvard University Press, 2000) and *The Making of Homeric Verse: The Collected Papers of Milman Parry*, edited by Adam Parry (Oxford: Oxford University Press, 1971).

2

TALKING OF GODS

ORIGIN STORIES

Time, birth, growth, decay – it is impossible to live in this world while unaware of continual flux and process. Add to this the certainty that we are not the first beings to inhabit our places, in an environment shaped by powerful uncontrollable forces of earth and atmosphere, and it soon becomes understandable why societies, ancient and modern, have invested in stories about origins. Such narratives explain how the present grows out of the past. They can include tales about the beginnings of the physical universe, or about human institutions. Why is that mountain located where it is? Why do we worship the gods in this particular ritual? The myths provide, not just an answer, but the overriding sense that for everything there *is* in fact a reason. Perhaps this sense is built into the very essence of successful narratives: first one thing happened and then *because* of that, another. As E. M. Forster once observed, "the king died and then the queen died is a story. The king died and then the queen died of grief is a plot." In the same way, myths provide more than a chronology; they assert causation as well as sequence, they "plot" the past.

At times the narratives might seem to conflict. Controversy still surrounds the relationship between two origin narratives on the American scene, for instance, one based on scientific reasoning and the other based on a literalist reading of the Old Testament. Whereas the former gives us strange stories of a universe that began billions of years ago in an enormous release of energy called the Big Bang, the effects of which are ongoing, the latter features a more familiar, wise, and all-powerful creator divinity who shapes the world and its inhabitants in six days. The role of human beings in these narratives has caused the greatest conflict. Are men and women the result of a long process of evolution, starting with stardust, the ultimate product of random processes of selection and adaptation, descendants of sea creatures by way of apes? Or are we children of Adam and Eve, the original human couple created by God in his own image and set in a paradise from which their sin of disobedience later got them ejected? These two contemporary narratives, with their respective roots in observation and belief, can help us approach three relevant points about myths in general, and ancient Greek myths in particular.

First, stories have consequences. Let's put it starkly. If my origin narrative holds that an exclusive divinity gave humans a mandate to populate the world and dominate creation (as Genesis 1:28 in the Hebrew Bible has long been interpreted), I may feel entitled to exploit natural resources, drill for oil, induce climate change, and exterminate species at will. If on the other hand your narrative says that you and fellow humans are not possessors of god-given privileges, but are incidental to more or less accidental processes of evolution, you may want to extend rights to other sentient beings like cats and chimpanzees (a proposition some recent philosophers like Peter Singer have explored). Alternatively, a fundamentalist believer in the Biblical narrative might hold all life, human and other, as precious, to be cultivated for the glory of God, rather than recklessly corrupted. And the believer in a scientific world-view might even maintain that ethics and morality, social cohesion and altruism, are themselves key parts of human evolution – implying that humans are responsible for their further progress as a species. In sum, the real-life consequences of our stories inevitably involve how we weave the human webs of religion, law, and social practices.

Second, origin stories are essentially about the *present*, even while they purport to describe the past. That is to say, the concerns of a given narrative are not historical in a modern sense – to capture the way things *really* happened – but instead reflect the needs and aspirations, institutions and powers, of the societies in which they were created and, in some cases, are still told. The narrative of origins in the Hebrew Bible, even though it crystallized in the sixth and fifth centuries BC, continues to be relevant because it reflects the faith and world-view of millions in communities of belief, in churches, with their structures and strictures, hierarchies and taboos. The story is relevant to the lives of its hearers and so survives.

We do not have to confine this point to Judaism or Christianity. Zoroastrian believers, for example, still tend holy fires in temples, even at the ground-zero point of twenty-first-century digital technology, Silicon Valley, just as their ancient Persian predecessors did. Their rituals parallel a complex origin story about the struggle between supernatural forces of light and darkness. The narrative is preserved in the *Gathas*, a series of hymns written in an Indo-Iranian language (Avestan), perhaps as early as 1000 BC. According to the Zoroastrian creation myth, a divinity of light and goodness, Ahura Mazda, created the universe and mankind, permeating them with bright white fire. Angra Mainyu, a rival god of darkness, made demons and poisonous creatures. The evil forces of the latter killed off the first, primeval human being and the first bull, but their deaths in turn produced useful plants as well as the first human couple. In the *yasna* ceremony, performed in the presence of the sacred fire, believers propitiate the holy guardians of the good elements of the world, in an effort to make all creation prosper and grow in righteousness, to foster and celebrate the fiery spark of life inside each creature. In other words, the cosmological narrative involving dueling gods of light and darkness works for Zoroastrians simultaneously on two levels. It is a commemoration of distant, one-time divine events. But it is also a justification for what worshipers enact in the here and now.

A different ancient narrative combines the two aspects we have just mentioned. The Babylonian creation epic *Enuma Elish* ("When on High") was recited every New Year. The performance was meant not merely to celebrate the divine kingship of Marduk, victor over more primitive gods, but to renew harmonious order in the world under his patronage (and that of his human representatives). In other words, retelling the mythic tale each year not only certified that Babylonian kings had a right to power – it was thought to serve (almost magically) to *keep* them in power. Here myth approaches what philosophers of language like J. L. Austin have called "performative utterances," those authoritative acts of declaration (like "I thee wed" or "I find the defendant guilty") that, by the very act of being uttered, make a certain state of affairs come about (getting married, going to jail).

With the Babylonian mythic narrative we come closer to the nature of the ancient Greek origin myths, not just (as we shall see shortly) because early Greek tale-tellers probably borrowed motifs from their much older Near Eastern neighbors. More obviously, neither the Greek origin stories nor the Babylonian are still cherished by communities of believers. There are no worshipers of Marduk or Zeus (with the exception of some neopagan revivalist fringe groups). The myths no longer have direct meaning for the societies in which they arose – unlike Genesis or the *Gathas* – as there is no historical continuity of religion between ancient Greece and contemporary culture in the same land, or archaic Babylon and modern Iraq. In both places, highly successful and international monotheistic religions (Orthodox Christianity and Islam, respectively) have replaced polytheistic predecessors.

It might seem that we have shifted with suspect ease from discussing "myth" to talk of "religion." This is an important question, related to the notoriously flexible semantic range of "myth," something we saw in the previous chapter. Without going into the full details of the debate over what separates the two (some of which we shall sample in Chapter 4, about theoretical approaches), suffice it to say that "myths" are very often "religious" narratives that people no longer believe. To put it another way, for an ancient Greek – let's say, a young woman in Sparta around 500 BC – the story of how Zeus came to power would form a portion of her religious environment. Its truth would be anchored in the facts of her daily life and landscape. In the marketplace she would see a sanctuary of Zeus Agoraios ("of the agora") close to that of his grandmother Gaia (Earth). She would know in what neighborhoods of the city Zeus was worshiped under various titles: "of fair wind"; the Olympian, the Giver of Order; the Most High; the Protector of Suppliants. And she would no doubt on festival-days visit shrines in surrounding villages and towns – that of Zeus the Dark One in Skotitas, or Zeus Giver of Wealth in Amyklai.

For every place in which the god was honored, there would be stories – why he got the cult-title, which famous people of the past had visited these exact spots. Some of the tales have been preserved, by writers like Pausanias who recorded his travels in the second century AD. But most such local or "epichoric" detail (from Greek "on the land") is lost. Instead, in the major poems that outline the origins of the gods and their honors, local versions have been shaded over in favor of stories that do not privilege particular spots or communities. Such versions with widespread appeal across the Greek world are called "Panhellenic" ("all-Greek"). Which brings us to the third important point of comparison with modern origin-myths.

Third, origin stories within the *same* culture are varied and contested. At first, this seems puzzling. Aren't origin narratives among the most venerable and important stories that a culture possesses? Wouldn't they reflect an age-old consensus? While we might expect there to be *one* narrative of how the world began for the Greeks, another for the people of ancient Israel, a third for the Babylonians, and so on, in actuality we have multiple versions from *each* place. Admittedly, each culture seems to have made an effort to combine and harmonize its competing stories in order to even out local differences or even radically different versions. It is well known that Genesis as we have it blends two somewhat different accounts of the creation of humans (Gen. 1:1–2:3 vs. 2:4–3:24). Sometimes, as in the ancient Near East, a cosmology reflects waves of invasions and takeovers, with each culture partially absorbing the myths and religious ideas of its predecessor. The Akkadians and Babylonians clearly integrated much earlier Sumerian divinities into their own myths.

In what follows, we'll trace one Panhellenic version of the origin of the universe and the gods that became canonical, for reasons still unclear, but most likely having to do with the spread of oral-poetic song-making as practiced in the eighth century BC and later (see Chapter 1). Then we'll look briefly at some more marginal but fascinating cosmologies. Finally, we'll examine some implications, for everyday Greek life, of origin tales and divine myths, more generally.

HESIOD'S *THEOGONY*

Composed about 700 BC, the long poem in dactylic hexameter verse (the style of Homeric epic – see Chapter 1) called the *Theogony* ("Birth of the Gods") bears the name of Hesiod. This poet represents himself, near the beginning of the narrative, as having obtained his information directly from the Muses themselves, goddesses of song, dance, fine speaking and music (the lattermost named after them: *Mousikê* signifies "the art of the Muses"). One day, while tending flocks on Mt. Helicon in his native Boiotia (between Delphi and Athens), Hesiod is visited by nine young women who hand him a laurel branch and breath into him a divine voice, bidding him to sing not only about all that has happened in the universe, but also, first and last, about themselves and about Zeus – father of the gods, and their own progenitor. By the time we get to this point, in fact, the poet has *already* sung a beautiful description of the goddesses bathing in a fountain on the top of Mt. Helicon and walking in procession down that slope by night, clothed in mist. In other words, the poem itself lets us see how Hesiod has fulfilled the bargain, even before we learn about his initiatory poetic encounter.

In performing the *Theogony*, then, Hesiod associates himself with the divine singers whose continual task is to "please the mind of Zeus" by praising him as father of gods and humans. The entire poem is, in fact, structured as a hymn to the chief god as sovereign of the cosmos. Because we know from other sources (like the long didactic poem *Works and Days*, also attributed to Hesiod) that the figure of the *basileus* or "king" was important in the imagination of archaic Greeks, the origin stories told in the *Theogony* take on additional mythic power. In short, the poem can be construed as support – even propaganda – for the notion of kingship, the human institution being directly linked to the divine king Zeus. It is not accidental, in this connection, that Calliope ("Fair-voice"), whom the poem names as one of the nine Muses, is said to favor kings with her gift of lovely speech, so that they persuade assembled crowds and resolve disputes (*Theogony* lines 79–93). In effect, Hesiod puts himself on a level with the class of kings, since both they and the poet are Muse-gifted masters of the word. On the other hand, by positioning himself as a praise-poet, he acknowledges subordination as client to powerful political patrons. So this is a poetic story with a particular spin that favors an aristocratic audience. Perhaps (at least at some stage of its growth) the *Theogony* was composed for kingly pleasure.

This dynamic interaction should make us think twice about the birth of the universe and gods as described in the *Theogony*. In brief, the cosmos develops toward a goal – the kingship of Zeus – and then stops. For the archaic Greek hearers of this origin story, something like evolution has occurred, but its results are no longer subject to further change, once Zeus has securely established himself on Olympus, mountainous home of the gods. The evolution that leads to this steady-state, furthermore, is marked by violent leaps. It is a story of generational conflict, and domestic abuse finally resolved by political savvy and frequent (albeit selective) divine impregnations. Not only does Zeus represent the product of a long series of regime changes. His new world order is marked by subtle and all-knowing intelligence, in stark contrast to the brute behavior of his predecessors.

Only a continuous, engaged reading of the poetic text will give you the totalizing and impressive effect of the *Theogony*. A summary, at least, can provide a sense of the evolutionary scheme I have been describing. The universe begins with a vast empty space, uncreated by any being, but itself the staging area for all further growth. This space is called Chaos – literally a "gap" (the Greek word did not yet signify wild movement or an uncontrollable situation). Next there "came to be" (without a creator figure) Earth, Tartarus (the dank, gloomy space beneath Earth) and Eros ("Desire"). The lattermost is necessary for the next steps that involve a series of sexual encounters: the mythic origin story quite logically posits an early principle of attraction to explain how various divine beings mated. Erebos ("Darkness") produces Aether ("Shining Sky") and Day. We might remark already that the sequence is not just cosmological but an everyday fact of Greek life, in which (as in that of many cultures) the new day began at sundown on the previous, or the day itself is thought of as having been conceived by the previous night. The same principle of Eros enables Earth, in the next major move, to mate with Sky (*Ouranos*, in Greek) – although, curiously, she had apparently borne this male being on her own, a motif of "parthenogenesis" we will encounter several times in Greek tales.

The poem specifies that Earth (an element and location as well as a goddess) was preparing herself to be "the ever immovable seat for the blessed gods." In short order, she bears (again, on her own) mountains (future homes for Nymphs) and sea. Then, she goes to bed with her husband/creation Sky. Their intercourse results in a group of a dozen gods who will come to be called Titans: among those that feature prominently in further stories are Rhea, Themis, Mnêmosynê and Okeanos.

It might seem strange that Earth has already borne Pontos (the sea), without intercourse, and now gives birth to what seems like a very

Figure 2.1 Eros (Desire) depicted as a handsome winged youth holding a lyre.
A cosmic principle that enables all sorts of productive mingling,
he is also in Classical representations the embodiment of intense
attraction between humans. Red-figure *lekythos*, c. 500 BC

Source: Eros, vase no. 13305, Red-figured lekythos (c. 500 BC). © Ashmolean Museum,
University of Oxford.

similar being, Okeanos. Like many doublets in the *Theogony*, one of
the pair (usually the latter-born) represents a more defined version of
the former. We can compare the twins Darkness and Night – one the
general phenomenon, the other a defined instance of it. Thus, Pontos
is barren and immeasurable, the open sea as perceived by terrified

early sailors. Okeanos (which gives us "Ocean"), on the other hand, designates a specific, bounded cosmic river running around the earth, which is imagined as a flat, rounded shape. When you travel to the extreme east or west, in Greek myths, you reach the same divinity; through encircling Okeanos, opposites converge.

After bearing three one-eyed Cyclopses and a set of three monstrous Hundred-handers, last of all Earth brings forth Kronos. At this point, the story becomes one of domestic abuse. Sky (naturally, to a human observer) is always on top of Earth. The myth depicts this as a violent experience. Ouranos never lets his children out of Earth, but instead hides them in her crevasses, so that she becomes intolerably burdened and seeks relief, literally to get Sky off her. She fashions a sickle, and in true folklore style, offers her youngest son the chance to undertake a manly deed: in this case, to unman her own oppressive husband by castration. Kronos tosses away the severed genitals of his father, but energy in cosmogonic myth is never wasted. Earth absorbs the bloody drops, eventually producing from them the Furies (Erinyes), Giants, and ash-trees.

Meanwhile, upon Pontos, the sea, the discarded organs generate a foamy froth, from which a beautiful goddess emerges: Aphrodite. The poet, as he often does, explains divine names by reference to the scenario. This goddess is "Aphrodite," because of the foam (aphros, in Greek); "Cytherea," since she first set foot on an island called Cythera; Cyprus-born, since that island was her next stop; and "laughter-loving since she came forth from the genitals." (This weird association relies on a Greek pun: the words for "smile" and "genitals" are homonyms.)

We can notice right off several varieties of connection in this mini "aitiology" or origin-explanation tale. First, the long-ago tale of islands that the goddess visited fits with the here-and-now facts concerning the location of her prominent worship sites in the Greek world. Second, the myth, at least in the Hesiodic telling, explains actual human behavior (laughing and smiling, seductive flirtation) as a reflex of a single primeval event. And third, the seemingly random detail (foam) turns out to play a major role in the conception (here quite literally) of a deity. This last point might lead us to imagine that the whole story of the castration and the immersion of the genitals in Pontos has been backward-engineered from a folk-etymology in archaic Greece. Why does "Aphrodite" have a name that sounds like foam, you ask? Let me tell you a story ... The Titans themselves, produced just before the love-goddess, were given their group nickname by their hateful father Kronos because they engaged in "straining" (*titainontas*) to do an evil deed (in his opinion), for which he vowed vengeance. Names mirror essences.

The mention of the overwhelming force of sexual attraction embodied in Aphrodite prompts the *Theogony* poet next to catalogue other powers arising in this primeval era, such as the Children of Night (Doom, Death, Sleep, Dreams, Blame, Pain, Old Age) and the famous Fates: Klotho (Spinner), Lachesis (Apportioning), and Atropos (Not-turning-back). Night's grandchildren, by her daughter Strife, include Labor, Forgetfulness, Hunger, Battles, Slaughters, Lies, Disputes, and Oath. The mythic logic at work here consists in associating forces and emotions that bear a resemblance to one another and presenting them as related genealogically. While the idea of a family of gods feels familiar to us (largely because Western culture grew up on Greek myth), the further idea that *all* phenomena, from light and dark to work and lying, are genetically akin strikes us as both bizarre but also prescient, like an early realization of the neurological and chemical basis of psychological states. "Oath" might seem an outlier in such company, but here another brand of logic kicks in: if something exists that demands a choice by humans – such as keeping an oath or breaking it – then the institution itself can be perceived as having two sides. Perhaps the same sort of logic underlies an even odder inclusion among Night's daughters, the Hesperides, divine keepers of golden apples and their trees that grow beyond Okeanos (lines 215–16). After all, the very existence of this unattainable fruit can be seen as a lure to travel beyond human boundaries, something only heroes, like Heracles, can successfully do. The Apple of Discord that started the Trojan War (by way of the Judgement of Paris) supposedly came from the Hesperides' orchard. Then again, the association of golden apples with Night might just have resulted from the observation that the sun sets in the west.

Pontos, the open sea, also populates the world of divinities, first bringing forth the "old man" Nereus, an infallible prophet, who then mates with a daughter of Okeanos to produce fifty "Nereids," whose names (all of them dutifully catalogued by Hesiod) reflect aspects of the sea. (Rivers, on the other hand, all come from the mating of Okeanos with his Titan sister Tethys.) Winds and the Gorgons also descend ultimately from Pontos. Of the latter,

Medusa will end up being decapitated by Perseus. In a re-run of the Kronos castration, this severing leads to birth as well, that of the magic horse Pegasus and a male divinity Chrysaor (Golden Dirk) who in turn begets the three-headed Geryoneus, a monster eventually overcome by Heracles in his journeys to the far West. These intrusions of the heroes of a later generation into Hesiod's account of primeval origins remind us that the world of hero-worship, a custom very much alive in the archaic and Classical Greek world, contributed to the shaping of origin myths. If heroes must overcome monsters, the latter have to have come from some frightful distant source to make them truly scary. Cosmogony fills this niche with the extended families of Night and Sea. Other threatening figures like the snake-woman Echidna, Cerberus the dog of Hades, the Hydra, the Chimaera and the Sphinx that threatens Thebes are said all to be akin.

Once these dangerous aspects of the world are established, the stage is set for the next violent outbreak within the immediate family of Earth and Sky. The myth of the next generation seems to be grappling with the psychological insight that abused children become abusive adults. Kronos, the heroic young Titan who saved his mother from her overbearing husband, now in turn marries Rhea, his sister, but then (like his father) threatens his own offspring, swallowing each in turn as it is born. The sisters Hestia, Demeter, and Hera, with their brothers Hades and Poseidon, all suffer this indignity. This time, the oppressed wife herself solves the problem. On the advice of her mother Earth, Rhea hides her last baby in a cave in Crete, presenting her husband with a swaddled–up stone instead of his real son. When he gulps it down, Kronos vomits up the rest of his children. This very stone, says Hesiod, was subsequently placed in Apollo's sanctuary at Delphi where it remains – once more we see contemporary worship tied mythically with the deep past.

After two generations, we finally arrive at the heroic career of Zeus. The god's successful rule depends on two key factors. First, he controls the terrifying weapons of weather. And second, he is a consummate politician. The two are related. One of his first moves on maturing is to free his uncles, whom their father Ouranos had bound beneath the earth. They reward Zeus with thunder and lightning. By promising another marginalized group, the Hundred-handers, a role in his regime Zeus recruits them to fight against the Titans. His subsequent total victory culminates in

Figure 2.2 Kronos (Saturn) devouring one of his sons. Unlike the Hesiodic
            version, and an earlier painting by Rubens, this depiction by
            the aging Francisco de Goya (painted on a wall of his house, c.
            1819–1823) seems to feature an older child rather than an infant

Source: ART71401 Goya, Saturn devouring one of his sons. From the series of "Black
Paintings," 1819–1823. Museo del Prado, Madrid, Spain. Photo Credit: Erich Lessing/
Art Resource, NY.

a spectacular blasting of the monstrous Typhoeus, of whom all that
remains are destructive, random winds.

King of the gods at last, Zeus makes one more political decision to
ensure that his reign will be eternal. He takes wives. Mêtis (Wisdom)

was the first. But because a prophecy foretold their child would be mightier than its father, Zeus takes the precaution of swallowing the pregnant mother. This enables him to have a constant wise advisor always on his side – literally, *inside*. But as energy is never lost in these origin myths, the pregnancy of Mêtis has to run its course. The result is Athena, who is born out of the head of Zeus. A series of subsequent marriages makes Zeus the father of the Seasons (*Horae*). Rather than representing stages of the year, these goddesses stand for principles of cosmic harmony: *Eunomia* (Lawfulness), *Dikê* (Justice), and *Eirênê* (Peace). He also fathers life-enhancing divinities like the Graces and well-known figures like Persephone (by his sister Demeter), the twins Apollo and Artemis (by Lêto), and Ares the war-god, along with Hêbê (Eternal Youth) and Eileithyia (goddess of childbirth), all by his ultimate official spouse Hera. A series of further dalliances, for which Zeus gains quite a reputation, produces Dionysos (by Semele); Hermes (by the nymph Maia) and Heracles (by the moral woman Alkmênê), the hero who will eventually be rewarded with Hêbê as his own wife, on the completion of his painful labors.

The origin myths contained in the *Theogony* thus segue seamlessly from the world of gods into that of heroes. These semi-divine beings (the focus of the next chapter) in turn channel the divine DNA of the Olympians into the circulation of ordinary Greek life. After all, proud rulers or leading families of city-states, even in historical times, traced their ancestry to such descendants of Zeus (or a few other gods). In this way, the activity of the gods has a direct influence on the structure of human communities. But there is an even more significant one-time mythic event that determines how all humans – no matter what their ancestry – will eventually live. This is the match of wits between Zeus and his cousin Prometheus, a son of the Titan Iapetos. (His brother was Atlas, whom Zeus tasked with holding up the sky on his shoulders.) It goes like this: in the early days of the rule by Zeus, humans and gods regularly met and dined together. The scenario makes us think of the blissful Garden of Eden period in Genesis, before the Fall. Prometheus (whose name was interpreted by Greeks to mean "forethought") took it upon himself to trick Zeus after dividing up an ox he had killed for the shared meal. He placed the tasty innards inside an unattractive covering of skin, and meanwhile hid the ox's bones inside an appealing layer of meat and fat. Have your pick of the two portions, he told Zeus. The chief god chose the bones-inside-fat package and then, angered by the deception, withdrew the element of fire from humans (ensuring no such further deceptive cookery events). In a tit-for-tat move, Prometheus steals fire back while Zeus is distracted; in turn Zeus produces a double punishment. He orders Prometheus to be fettered to a pillar in the distant Caucasus Mountains, where his immortal liver will be gnawed each day by an eagle (Zeus' favorite bird) only to grow back each night. Then, he orders his craftsman son Hephaestus to fabricate out of earth a "beautiful bad thing" (*kalon kakon*), a maiden adorned with all sorts of gifts by the other gods – hence her name Pandora ("all gifts"). The plan is to inflict harm on mankind, the friends of Prometheus. Luckily for Zeus, his cousin has a dumber brother Epimetheus (Afterthought) who willingly takes the crafted woman into his house. She in turn has been provided with a large storage jar, a *pithos* (not a "box" or *pyxis* – a reinterpretation stemming from a later mistranslation of the text in the Renaissance). Out of curiosity she opens the jar and unwittingly releases its evil contents: death-causing disease and all sorts of pain. Only Hope (*Elpis*) lingers inside the lid – an ambiguous detail that might mean Hope itself still lives, for mankind, but is at the same time itself an evil.

In sum, the conditions of mortal life are finally determined by this big-bang mythic event. First, the "tribe of women" (as Hesiod styles it) comes to exist. Like its archetype, according to this traditionally misogynistic text, women are "a great woe for mortals, companions not in hateful baneful poverty but only in luxury," drone-like creatures who remain inside consuming the worker bees' honey. (Hesiod like most ancients was confused about facts of entomology.) But at the same time, the text says (like the hoary joke), "you can't live without 'em." Women cause mortal men to work, a woman introduced suffering into the world (compare Adam and Eve) – but if you don't marry a woman, your male line dies out and you have no one to take care of you or farm the fields. So marriage and agricultural work are two intertwined inventions.

Second, the form of the central Greek religious ritual is established forever by the deceptive craft of Prometheus. In every major meat sacrifice, part of the animal is set aside for the gods, most often bones, and burnt on the altar, while the edible parts are cooked and consumed. In this way, the Prometheus origin story functions as the aitiological explanation for sacrificial procedure. But, as we have

Figure 2.3 Pandora (All Gifts), the unwitting agent for the revenge of Zeus against his cousin and rival Prometheus. From the box she is opening evil and disease escape. For this work of 1871 the Victorian painter Dante Gabriel Rossetti took as his model Jane (Burden) Morris, the wife of a fellow pre-Raphaelite, William Morris

seen, it is far more complex and multifunctional. Sacrifice of oxen, goats, or sheep involves feeding and raising animals; which means agriculture; which is tied to marriage. The whole system coheres, and it all goes back to a one-off whim on the part of a rebellious trickster divinity. In world mythology, tricksters like Loki among the Norse, Coyote among Native American tribes, and Maui, for the Hawaiians, fill similar functions.

OTHER ORIGIN MYTHS

The *Theogony* came to be taken as the canonical story of how the gods originated and the current world took shape at their command. But what about humans? Where did they come from? It happens that Prometheus appears prominently in other versions as the direct helper or even primary creator of men and women. As often occurs in studying mythology, we cannot determine whether these versions are as old as the stories found in Hesiod, but simply had not been recorded until later, or whether the source that transmits the tales just made them up. In the first version to be considered, the "source" is already distanced because the teller is Protagoras (a fifth-century BC "sophist," a professional itinerant teacher of all sorts of skills, for money). But this "Protagoras" from whom we get the myth is in turn a stylized version of the real one, in a dialogue by the philosopher Plato (427–347 BC) that purports to record a conversation with his own mentor, Socrates (c. 470–399 BC). What is more, both Socrates and Plato were well-known opponents of the swarm of sophists that descended on Athens in their time. All this makes us more cautious about attributing the origin tale to age-old tradition. On the other hand, we have little evidence to show that even Hesiod's (eventually standard) *Theogony* myths were more than just the creation of a few poets.

Protagoras, in the Platonic dialogue bearing his name, wants to argue that virtue can be taught (indeed, it's one of the lessons he professes to convey). In order to do so, he tells a story (calling it a *muthos*). Once, the gods made mortal creatures (humans and animals, together) out of earth and fire, and then asked Prometheus and his brother to give them various capacities and powers. Epimetheus took on the distribution, to various creatures giving different features such as wings, hooves, hides, speed, strength, and so forth. Lacking the forward-planning ability of his gifted brother, however, Epimetheus only realized after finishing with the animals that there were no distinctive features left over for humans. So Prometheus stole fire from Hephaestus and technical skills from Athena, which he then provided to the defenseless mortals to ensure their survival. Zeus tops off the human condition by having Hermes distribute a sense of justice to all. People have to be taught how to practice it, however.

It was Prometheus himself who created humans, according to another version, attested widely in sources later than the *Theogony*. This story was supported by local beliefs, it seems. According to the travel-writer Pausanias (10.4.4), there existed in a ravine at Panopeus (in central Greece) two huge stones that smelled like human skin. The people of the district claimed that these were leftover bits of the clay from which Prometheus fashioned humanity. Significantly, an origin myth recounted in another long poem by Hesiod, *Works and Days*, seems to intentionally evade this Promethean invention of mankind and to counterpoint it instead with a competing version. Instead of clay, people are made of metal. And instead of Prometheus, it is Zeus or unnamed immortals who make them. In the "Myth of the Five Ages" the gods at the time of Kronos made, first, a Golden race that lived like immortals, free from pain and the labor of producing food. After their long lives ended, a Silver race was created, a foolish generation that failed to worship the Olympians and so was done away with. Zeus himself made the third race, a Bronze generation devoted to war that ended up killing each other. The fourth race has no metal equivalent: it comprises demigods called heroes, (to be discussed further in Chapter 3). They, too, perish in a series of wars. The final age is that of Iron, in which Hesiod places himself and his contemporaries, prone to injustice and violence, and doomed, in Hesiod's prophetic vision, to eventually drive out all sense of shame and righteous indignation (*Nemesis*). Clearly, this myth of origins is constructed to spell out the moral lesson of the poem, which is in large part a tract instructing Hesiod's brother about the benefits of thrift, work, and fair dealing.

Yet another version of the origin of human beings occurs in a complex of marginally attested myths related to the god Dionysos and the semi-divine singer and lyre player, Orpheus. Zeus lay with his own daughter, Persephone, according to this version (which the people of Crete favored, saying it happened there), and she gave birth to the god Dionysos. Already, the tale diverges from the better-known version, in which Zeus fathered the god with Semele, the daughter of Cadmus in Thebes, a woman he later incinerated, snatching the prematurely born Dionysos from her womb. In the less canonical version, the child god, known also as Zagreus, is lured away by the Titans, at the urging of a jealous Hera, killed, torn apart, and eaten. Athena manages to save the heart of Dionysos/Zagreus, and he is later regenerated. But Zeus meanwhile incinerates the Titans, and it is from their ashes that mankind is created.

The tie-in to Orpheus comes in several ways. First, it was said that the mythical singer performed this tale of human origins. Theogonic poetry and hymns attributed to Orpheus circulated in antiquity. Second, Orpheus himself, in other stories, was said to have been killed and torn apart by women of Thrace, either because they were frenzied worshipers of Dionysos, or because, by inventing homosexuality he distracted their husbands. Third, like Dionysos (who in some versions rescued his mother Semele) and Persephone (abducted by Hades but allowed to re-visit earth each year), Orpheus, too, was said to have gone to the underworld and returned – albeit empty-handed, since he failed to retrieve his dead wife Eurydice.

When it comes to this offbeat version of Zagreus and humans made from soot, we happen to have some sense of the social and religious context in which the myth arose. As early as the sixth century BC, groups of ritual experts called "Orphics," who seem to have been involved as well with worship of Dionysos, roamed the Greek-speaking world offering purification and a happy afterlife if one followed the wisdom of their hero Orpheus. Along with ascetic practices, they abstained from meat (probably due to a belief in transmigration of souls – but odd, in the view of the ox-sacrificing majority of Greeks). And they encouraged the spread of ritual tablets for the afterlife. These miniature texts inscribed on gold leaf have been discovered in graves from the Black Sea area all the way to Sicily. In poetic verses, they instruct the deceased about how he or she should behave on arrival in the underworld, offering such consolation as "Now you have died and now you have been born, thrice happy one, on the same day. Tell Persephone [mistress of the underworld] that the Bacchic One himself released you." In short, from such materials we can sense the rich and heady mix of ritual, mythic tales, customs, song traditions, and cosmogony that swirled around better-attested stories of origins. Orphic beliefs obviously motivated some Greeks to carry out certain rituals. But the Hesiodic story of the rise of Zeus and his duel with Prometheus also served to motivate and validate a range of beliefs and behaviors, whether endorsing kingship and poetry or underlining the primeval rationale for meat sacrifice. One cannot draw a sharp line between "literary" and "cult" myths of origin.

WHERE GODS COME FROM

How did the Greeks ever come to imagine the gods at all in the ways they did? There are essentially three answers, none of which is exclusively the right one: they inherited the notions; they borrowed them; and they made them up. Myth is broad enough to accommodate all three.

Let's begin with borrowing, because it has been most discussed in recent scholarly debates. Explorations during the nineteenth century uncovered inscriptions in "cuneiform" writing (with signs made by wedge-shaped indentations) at Nimrud, Babylon and other cities in Mesopotamia (modern Iraq). By mid-century, aided by a trilingual inscription containing one already known language (Persian), these began to be deciphered, revealing a variety of ancient languages and astounding texts. For example, a myth about a primeval universal flood, found in 1872 in a collection of cuneiform texts from Nineveh, immediately prompted comparisons with the Biblical story of Noah and the Greek tale about the deluge-survivors Pyrrha and Deucalion (son of Prometheus). With the decipherment in the early twentieth century of thousands of texts found in another ancient cultural center, the empire of the Hittites centered in Anatolia (modern Turkey), it became clear that Greek origin myths contained uncanny resemblances to those of their much older neighbors to the east. It was implausible that such close likeness was due to chance; also, the direction of borrowing had to be from East to West. After all, the Greeks, as archaeology indicates, were relative newcomers to their lands, infiltrating the Balkans from the north and east around 2000 BC, whereas the Sumerians had flourished in Mesopotamia during the fourth millennium BC, the Hurrians in Anatolia a thousand years later, and the Hittites, Akkadians, and Assyrians who displaced or absorbed these earlier peoples, during the second millennium BC.

Two stories in particular foreshadow Hesiod's *Theogony*. First, the Babylonian creation story *Enuma Elish* (mentioned above) describes how the gods arose from intercourse between primeval elements. Apsu, divinity of sweet waters, mingled with Tiamat, the female salt water. An intervening generation of gods (mud or slime) produces in turn Sky and Earth, who then generate Anu, a sky god. His son is a trickster figure, named Ea (equivalent to Enki in the related literature of the Sumerians, the oldest written myths found to date). Like Ouranos and Kronos, Apsu makes an attempt to do away with the younger gods (their noise disturbs his sleep). But Ea, hearing the plot, kills him and takes over the symbols of sovereignty. He fathers the god Marduk, who is associated with storms. Tiamat, his great-grandmother, like Gaia in Hesiod (an elemental elder goddess) produces hybrid monster opponents. The young god kills these and cleaves her in two, then makes himself patron divinity of Babylon and chief of the pantheon. He establishes order through setting up the constellations, introducing a calendar, and regulating streams of water. On the whole, the schema of an evolutionary struggle for kingship recalls the Hesiodic narrative, albeit with more exuberant detail and extravagant numbers (e.g. the existence of 600 minor gods). Unlike the *Theogony*, the Babylonian origin epic tells of the creation of humankind, from clay and the blood of a defeated rebel god.

From the Hittite tradition in Anatolia comes another myth about royal succession in which Alalu is defeated by Anu and exiled to the underworld. Anu then yields to Kumarbi (who bites off his genitals), but himself is finally overcome by a weather god named Teshub. As some names show (e.g. Anu, the Babylonian sky god), the Hittite "kingship in Heaven" story has already undergone Mesopotamian influence – scribes trained in Akkadian are known to have lived at Hattusa, the second-millennium Hittite capital (modern Boğazkale, in northern Turkey). This tale of violent overthrows is filled out by the "Song of Ullikummi," concerning Teshub's battle against a stone monster begotten by the resentful Kumarbi. At the urging of Ea (another borrowed Babylonian god), Teshub employs an ancient cutting tool to separate Ullikummi from an Atlas-like sky-supporter on which the monster stands. (Recall the sickle used by Kronos against his father and Zeus' defeat of Typhoeus.)

In the light of these eastern narratives, Hesiod's *Theogony*, dating from around 700 BC, looks like an artful combination of much older non-Greek themes and motifs. Borrowing was not unlikely, given trade exchanges in the Bronze Age among Egypt, Mesopotamia,

Crete, Cyprus, Asia Minor and the coastal cities of what are now
Syria and Lebanon. After all, the Greek alphabet itself is obviously
borrowed from the Phoenician variety of a Semitic writing system (perhaps around 900 BC). Furthermore, the Greek pantheon of
divinities is clearly a patchwork construction of various borrowings.
Apollo and Artemis, the divine twin children of Zeus and Leto, bear
strong eastern traits, with the former resembling a Semitic plague god
(Resheph) and the latter the widely attested figure of the Mistress of
Animals. Even by Hesiod's account, Aphrodite comes from Cyprus
(the seat of her greatest worship throughout antiquity). The goddess
of love is linked with eastern counterparts such as the Phoenician
Astarte and the Akkadian Ishtar. Demeter, mother of Persephone, a
divinity of fertility whose angry withdrawal afflicts mortals, recalls
a Hittite story dating to the fifteenth century BC, told of a male
god, Telepinu, son of the mother of all gods. (A possible etymol-
ogy for Demeter is "Earth Mother.") The porous boundary between
Greek lands and those to the east later led to such openly acknowledged importations as the cult of the dying-and-resurrected Adonis
(favorite of Aphrodite) and the Great Mother, under such names as
Cybele and Dindymene. No doubt such inter-regional circulation of
religious thinking had long been operative.

Yet this seems quite strange. Is it possible that the migrating Greeks
arrived at the shores of the Aegean without any gods or myths of their
own? What role did cultural inheritance and continuity play? In fact,
we can be certain that at least a few gods must already have been known
to the Greeks, and stories told about them, long before they entered
into what would become their homeland. The evidence, in this case,
comes not from ancient texts but from a reconstructed language and
society called "Indo-European." Starting in the late eighteenth century,
scholars noticed the unusual similarities among Sanskrit, the classical language of India; Latin; Greek; and the oldest members of such
language families as Celtic (Irish, Welsh, etc.), Slavic (Russian, Polish,
etc.), and Germanic (including English). By meticulous comparison
of words and the formulation of rules for sound-changes, they grad-
ually refined the model of an ancient prototype from which all these
tongues descended. The reconstruction relies on the assumption that
only an inherited "genetic" relationship could explain the extremely
close resemblances between linguistic structures like verb and noun
systems. The idea is that basic items (numbers, names of animals, kin

terms) were neither invented by each language nor borrowed one from another, but that all naturally accompanied the populations that spoke the original "Indo-European" dialects, who spread out from a central point (probably southern Russia) around 3000 BC and went east to India and west as far as Ireland. Not only words but also cultural concepts – the importance of "fame" through poetry, and a religious pantheon – must have travelled with the migrating groups. Thus, it can be proposed on linguistic grounds that the Greek god "Zeus" is the "same" divinity as Latin *Ju-piter* (literally "sky-father" – a compound word), which matches Sanskrit *dyaus pitā*, as well as the Irish word *dia* ("god"), the Latin word *dies* ("day") and Greek adjective *dios* "shining." These all can be traced to an Indo-European word-root **dyew-* meaning "shining" (the asterisk is a convention indicating that the root is hypothetical, not written in any actual text).

Among the few Indo-European divinities clearly surviving in Greek culture are Dawn (*Eos*, linguistically related to Latin *Aurora* and Sanskrit *Uṣās*), the Sun (*Helios*), and the twins Castor and Polydeukes (whose function, but not name, matches the Sanskrit *Aśvinī*). Religious notions like purity, holiness, awe, and sacrifice also show resemblances in vocabulary across Indo-European language groups. What we do not know is the extent to which plotlines that were originally inherited from the shared mother-culture were later re-applied by Greeks to gods and heroes whom they found onsite when immigrating onto the southern Balkans and the shores of the Aegean. Probably their indigenous myths about gods blended over centuries with stories they picked up from the "Minoans" (the pre-Greek people living on Crete up to the mid-second millennium) and others in their new locales. Or, folktales common to several Indo-European groups may have been reshaped into more "realistic" epic narratives, like the tale of the Trojan War. The Classicist Lowell Edmunds has traced one such Indo-European story-pattern, the "Abduction of the Beautiful Wife," in the Helen of Troy tale, the figure of Sita in the Indic epic *Ramayana*, the abduction of Draupadi in the *Mahabharata*, and several Old Irish tales that eventually gave rise to the story of Guinevere, wife of King Arthur.

The third possibility for explaining the shape of divine myths in Greek is that they were simply made up by poets and storytellers. There is a kernel of truth in this, since those who study folklore hold that it is "traditional" to innovate. In other words, every rep-etition of a tale, especially in a largely oral culture, involves a new twist by the teller, meant to hold and impress each new audience.

In practice, however, this inherent tendency toward making it new parallels a tendency to preserve the most successful or respected portions of an older composition – sometimes reaching back many centuries. The paradoxical result is that a tale about the rise of Zeus and his divine compatriots, the Olympians, or about the abduction of Helen, might be both a new creation (as in Hesiod's poetic masterpiece, the *Theogony*), maybe borrowing attractive or scary ideas from the Near East, in an effort to outdo other performing poets, *and* yet be built on ancient templates of story-patterns reaching back to the Indo-Europeans. This complex blend of borrowing, innovation, and inheritance was already envisioned by the Greek historian of the Persian Wars, Herodotus, writing in the later fifth century BC. In his lengthy account of the Egyptians, in Book Two of the *Histories*, Herodotus states: "In fact, the names of nearly all the [Greek] gods came to Hellas [Greece] from Egypt. For I am convinced by inquiry that they have come from foreign parts, and I believe that they came chiefly from Egypt" (Herodotus, 2.50.1). Yet, a few pages later, he writes:

> But whence each of the gods came to be, or whether all had always been, and how they appeared in form, they [The Greeks] did not know until yesterday or the day before, so to speak; for I suppose Hesiod and Homer flourished not more than four hundred years earlier than I; and these are the ones who taught the Greeks the genesis of the gods, and gave the gods their titles, and determined their spheres and functions, and described their outward forms.

In other words, from the point of view of the cultural historian, the Greeks *inherited* the idea of gods; *borrowed* their names from what they thought were Egyptian equivalent gods; and *created* – quite late in the game – the look and feel of the divinities by way of newly made stories and poems. Herodotus' analysis is, remarkably, most likely to be the closest to reality (although Egypt was not the only source for borrowings).

WHAT ARE GODS GOOD FOR?

As we have seen so far, "myth," when it comes to stories about divine beings acting in the universe, blends quickly into "religion." But the two are not completely overlapping areas. Because creative artists like poets and vase-painters could stylize and invent details or even new episodes to enhance their narratives about gods, the resulting mythic material is more flexible and individualized than iron-clad dogmas set out in a sacred book that might make exclusive claims to spiritual truths. We are more familiar with the latter in the sacred texts of modern monotheistic religions, whether Christian, Jewish or Muslim. It is difficult to grasp how fantastic tales of divine doings – like Zeus' affairs or the descent of Orpheus to the underworld – can simultaneously be invested with belief, provide relevance for rituals, and yet also be experienced as entertainment. And yet that is precisely the triple power that ancient Greek myths seem to have possessed. In this final section of the chapter, I'll take for granted the entertainment value of myths while sampling two categories of deeper meaning: the importance of myths to individuals and to city-state society. A final coda will then blur these lines.

The life-stages of an individual in ancient Greece would resonate with stories of the gods, ripe with psychological and social meanings. In her labor pains, a mother might call on Eileithyia, the goddess of childbirth, maybe recalling the role that this daughter of Hera played in the story of Heracles (when she slowed his birth process and sped up that of his baby cousin Eurystheus). The ceremonies of the *amphidromia* (when a father ritually carried his newborn around the hearth) would recall the story of how the goddess Demeter acted as a nursemaid to a royal infant (whom she tried to immortalize by dipping into fire). Having been immersed in a world of stories throughout childhood, those who reached puberty would experience their formal initiation into adulthood in rituals closely tied to myths. Well-born girls in Athenian territory, for example, spent time at the shrine of Artemis in Brauron, a coastal town to the east of the city. There they performed ritual tasks and also participated in running and athletic events, in imitation of their patroness. Girls not yet "tamed" by marriage (as the Greek metaphor saw it) were properly in the realm of the goddess, just like wild animals. A whole complex of tales surrounding the goddess Artemis, about Actaeon and Orion (hunters whom Artemis killed in defense of her virginity or that of her companions) would evoke for them the threat of male sexuality. On the other hand, the story of her friend the nymph Callisto, driven away by Artemis when she was found to be pregnant by Zeus, underlined how, once they moved into the realm of Aphrodite (sex and marriage) girls had to abandon that of Artemis. In myth, when Artemis presides over the sacrifice of

Agamemnon's daughter Iphigenia, whose death she commanded, we get a dramatic exaggeration of the "social death" that the initiated undergo in moving from one status (girlhood) to another. The doublings of the tale (fatal in the imaginary, while a minor ordeal in real life) is reflected in the myth's dual outcomes, because another version held that Iphigenia (like Abraham's son Isaac in Genesis) was rescued by the goddess and replaced at the last moment by a sacrificial animal.

For young men reaching adulthood, Apollo presided over initiation. Like his sister, he was represented in myth as causing death for various followers or companions. The young man Hyacinthus, for instance, hit accidentally by Apollo while being taught to throw the discus, gave his name to a flower that sprang from his blood. His relationship to Apollo was marked by the god's important yearly festival at Amyklai in Spartan territory. Most prominent among Apollo's victims was Achilles, the best of the Greek warriors at Troy, whom the god eventually killed, with assistance from the mortal Paris. Handsome, with unshorn hair, an expert at war and music-making, Achilles came dangerously close in appearance and skills to Apollo, more than a semi-mortal might dare. The logic of myth, and the "anthropomorphic" (human-appearing) nature of the Greek gods ensured that such similarity between divinities and heroes led to antagonism. In real life, meanwhile, young men would emulate and serve Apollo, modeling themselves on this perfect expression of (divine) "manhood." Of course, Apollo's overseeing of male transitions to adult status was not his sole role. But a young Greek might associate the god's ability to foresee the future, to give forth oracles at Delphi (empowered by his father Zeus), to dispatch colonizers, and to lead the Muses in song and dance as interrelated aspects of his function as harmonizer, director, and guide. Once more, "myth" goes along with a host of other activities grounded in social life.

The gods were also deeply embedded in the daily life of city-states, overarching the experience of individuals. Thus, a plethora of stories related how Poseidon, Athena, Apollo, Hera, Artemis or Zeus came to be the protectors of specific communities. Athena defeated Poseidon in a gift-giving duel to win naming rights in her city, Athens. The island of Rhodes was sacred to Helios, with myths telling how he was awarded its namesake nymph by Zeus. The great third-century BC bronze "colossus" astride the harbor entrance at Rhodes – 105 feet high, and one of the Seven Wonders of the ancient world – represented this god of the sun. Beyond city patronage, divinities and heroes were important as guarantors or inventors of social structure within communities. At Athens, about which we have the most evidence, the ten fundamental "tribes" through which democratic participation was first organized in the late sixth century BC were named after ten local heroes, mostly mythical kings. Sacrifices to Zeus, Athena, Demeter, and a number of lesser divinities were occasions to highlight people's ranks in the social hierarchy, as at the great procession in the festival of the Panathenaia that marked every Athenian new year (subject of the superb fifth-century BC sculpted frieze from the Parthenon temple, now exhibited mostly in the British Museum).

Heroes' deeds and careers were alluded to in dozens of ways in the city's institutions. A gymnasium in the Kynosarges district, reserved for bastard sons, was dedicated to Heracles, since he himself was Zeus's son by a woman other than Hera. The historical synthesizing of villages around Athens into a greater political whole was attributed to Theseus, son of Poseidon (and/or Aegeus). One could not walk around the area of the Acropolis without seeing shrines to Pan, the Nymphs, Hephaestus, Aphrodite, Artemis, Victory (*Nikê*), or the Twelve Gods, each evoking a string of myths. In this way, the inhabitants of Athens were constantly subjected to the possibilities and prohibitions transmitted by a world of stories. The same applied to every other Greek community.

Some myths were particularly useful in enabling the Greeks to think about the boundaries and bridges between gods and humans, individuals and society. Prime among these must be that of Eros – "Desire." A son of Chaos, according to the *Theogony*, this beautiful winged young god was worshiped at sanctuaries and festivals throughout the Greek world. (Only in later antiquity did he degenerate into the pudgy mischievous toddler we know as Cupid, his Roman name.) In classical Greece, Eros presided not just over erotic ties between men and women, but over all social bonds, including male homoerotic relations – an important feature of upper-class Athenian life. In gymnasium statues, represented on the bases of "herms" (rough blocks with a head of Hermes and an erect phallos), or painted on exquisite Athenian pottery, Eros was everywhere. Nor were the Athenians alone in celebrating his powers. Spartans sacrificed to Eros before battle, a sign of their faith in the power of male bonding between warriors. The Thebans actually deployed a sacred band of 150 pairs of fighter-lovers in the fourth century BC.

The dialogue *Symposium*, written by the philosopher Plato around 380 BC, displays the philosopher's typical brilliance at mythologizing. Some of the motifs and themes we can recognize also in other sources, but Plato nevertheless sketches a fresh and entrancing picture that seeks to reconcile the contradictory aspects of Eros – the intensely individual experience of love and the socially oriented, community-building power that leads people to strive for higher things. Plato puts into the mouth of Socrates a description of Eros that his mentor, in turn, claims to have heard from a woman with prophetic skills called Diotima (*Symp*. 201d–212a). Eros is neither beautiful nor ugly, neither god nor mortal, but an intermediary, she tells him, the son of Poverty and Resourcefulness, "a famous hunter, always weaving some stratagem; desirous and competent of wisdom, throughout life ensuing the truth; a master of jugglery, witchcraft, and artful speech" (trans. W. R. M. Lamb). The myth of Eros which Socrates hands down to his audience becomes a profound meditation on how passionate desire can become the first step of an ascent that leads to the experience of the changeless reality that underlies all passing phenomena – the core of existence simultaneously good, beautiful and true. As with many myths, not just the formally philosophical, a fascinating story both conceals and reveals realities inaccessible to ordinary discourse. Myth, at this level, is a deeper form of language and of thought.

FURTHER READING

For a broad comparative perspective on origin myths, *A Dictionary of Creation Myths* (New York: Oxford University Press, 1994), compiled by David and Margaret Leeming, is a fine starting place. On such narratives in the Bible, Thomas L. Brodie provides a thorough introduction in *Genesis as Dialogue: A Literary, Historical, and Theological commentary* (New York: Oxford University Press, 2001).

The best introduction to Hesiod is Robert Lamberton's *Hesiod* (New Haven: Yale University Press, 1988), while the best recent text and translation are in the two Loeb Classical Library volumes, *Hesiod*, edited by Glenn Most (Cambridge, MA: Harvard University Press, 2006). The French scholar Jean-Pierre Vernant provides groundbreaking social analysis of the *Theogony* in *Myth and Thought among the Greeks* (London: Routledge & Kegan Paul, 1983). A striking and useful contrast to his Structuralist perspective is Richard Caldwell's

The Origin of the Gods: A Psychoanalytic Study of Greek Theogonic Myth (New York: Oxford University Press, 1989). On the notions of epichoric and Panhellenic applied to Hesiod, see Gregory Nagy, *Greek Mythology and Poetics* (Ithaca: Cornell University Press, 1990).

J. L. Austin's notion of speech-acts set forth in his classic *How To Do Things with Words* (2nd ed. by J. O. Urmson and Marina Sbisà, Cambridge, MA: Harvard University Press, 1975) has been applied by me to Greek myth in *The Language of Heroes: Speech and Performance in the Iliad* (Ithaca: Cornell University Press, 1989).

The Near Eastern sources for Hesiod's myths are examined, along with many other parallels to Greek literature, in Martin West, *The East Face of Helicon: West Asiatic Elements in Greek Poetry and Myth* (Oxford: Oxford University Press, 1999). Good translations of the original Mesopotamian texts are in Stephanie Dalley, *Myths from Mesopotamia: Creation, the Flood, Gilgamesh, and Others* (Oxford: Oxford University Press, 2000). The Indo-European heritage is examined by Joseph F. Nagy, in an important essay, "Hierarchy, Heroes, and Heads: Indo-European Structures in Greek Myth," in *Approaches to Greek Myth* (2nd ed. by Lowell Edmunds, Baltimore: Johns Hopkins University Press, 2014). On the Helen myth as part of a broader Indo-European folktale type, see Lowell Edmunds, *Stealing Helen: The Myth of the Abducted Wife in Comparative Perspective* (Princeton: Princeton University Press, 2015).

The functions of specific Greek myths, whether of origins or others, are addressed in Ken Dowden's *The Uses of Greek Mythology* (London: Routledge, 1992). The same author's *Death and the Maiden: Girls' Initiation Rites in Greek Mythology* (London: Routledge, 1989) analyzes the Artemis connection. On male initiation and myth, see David Dodd and Christopher A. Faraone (eds.) *Initiation in Ancient Greek Rituals and Narratives: New Critical Perspectives* (London: Routledge, 2013). The best starting point for study of any of the gods and goddesses mentioned in this chapter is Walter Burkert, *Greek Religion* (Cambridge, MA: Harvard University Press, 1985). On the Orphic gold tablets, see Fritz Graf and Sarah Iles Johnston, *Ritual Texts for the Afterlife: Orpheus and the Bacchic Gold Tablets* (New York: Routledge, 2007).

On Plato's mythologizing, in context, see Kathryn A. Morgan, *Myth and Philosophy from the Presocratics to Plato* (Cambridge: Cambridge University Press, 2000). Finally, the poet-Classicist Anne Carson has written brilliantly on the subject of Plato's *Symposium* and related Greek attempts to understand Desire in *Eros the Bittersweet: An Essay* (Princeton: Princeton University Press, 1986).

3

HEROIC DIMENSIONS

Like "myth," the modern word "hero" has developed a range of meanings and applications that can be distracting for someone who wants to get at the ancient Greek concept, and thus at the fuller meaning of hero myths. Consider how the word is used nowadays in ordinary English. Most frequently, it's a headline-writer's concept. A "hero" (or "heroine") is someone who dies trying to help other people. It's the young girl rescuing her family from a burning trailer or the elderly man who jumps in front of a train to save a child accidentally fallen on the tracks. Animals (usually it's dogs) are "heroes" when they alert their owners to danger or fight off threats (robbers, wild animals). Then, there are the members of certain professions whom it has become conventional to call "heroes" given their vigilance and willingness to take risks (again, the notion of protecting others is prominent): firefighters, police officers, ambulance drivers, and above all, the military (especially after the 9/11 attacks in the US).

We commemorate the sappers who built World War I tunnels as "heroic sewer rats of the Somme," and regularly use the phrase "war hero." On occasion, the latter usage is subjected to debate, usually in the context of a political race: was Senator X really a "hero" when he languished in a North Vietnamese prison for five years, instead of being shot on the front lines? Did Congressman Y really swim, heroically, all night to save his shipwrecked crew members? Does one have to die to be a "hero"? Does the word apply automatically to every war veteran? Only in electoral situations, it seems, does the general public begin wondering about the further implications of the otherwise breezily bandied-about term.

Evaluating the past and fantasizing about the present are two other modes of talk in which "heroism" comes up. Was Andrew Jackson or Teddy Roosevelt (or his cousin F. D. R.) a "hero" as president? Are the heroic reputations of Mother Teresa or Oskar Schindler deserved? Historians toss around the term without examining what it entails. On the other hand, everyone seems to understand what it takes to be a "superhero" (Batman, Spiderman, Superman, Wonder Woman, and hordes of others). Yet few seem to ask why already possessing a special power (ability to leap tall buildings at a single bound, etc.) translates into "heroism" since the possessor, apparently, is not really taking risks – even though he or she admittedly uses a given power to protect people.

Finally, a creeping trend to consider every person on earth a "hero," simply for getting through each day, was accelerated in the twentieth century by therapists, in league with Jungian psychologists (see Chapter 4) aided conveniently by the same entertainment industry that also holds up "superheroes" as beings far above our own lowly capacities. The result is summed up perfectly in a recent book by Adam Berger, *Every Guest Is a Hero: Disney's Theme Parks and the Magic of Mythic Storytelling* (BAC Publications, 2013). But if everyone can be a hero (or heroine) for one day and the price of admission to a theme park featuring wonderfully manufactured thrills ("imagineered" as Disney would put it), doesn't the term lose any real content? Ultimately, it becomes "heroic" to be a consumer.

Do we actually need a definition in order to investigate stories about Heracles, Achilles, Antigone and other Greek heroic figures? As we saw in the previous chapter, once we begin to explore Greek myths, it turns out that the essential difference between them and mere entertainment of the modern kind lies in their being embedded in cultural features that are vastly unlike the modern world's. Specifically, when it comes to myths about origins and gods the very notion of a divinity who has an extended family, who is immortal but nevertheless looks, feels, and acts like a (potentially violent) human, means that the narratives function on two levels. They are flexible, exciting tales; and they are also expressions of religious belief

Figure 3.1 "Uprising of the Spirit" (1994) by the Mexican artist Enrique Chagoya
evokes the encounter of indigenous people and colonizing Europeans
in his home country, as embodied in iconic culture heroes (Superman
versus the fifteenth-century native warrior Nezahualcoyotl). In the
ancient Mediterranean, one region's hero often was a villain in the
imagination of other communities

Source: ART407686 Chagoya, Enrique (b. 1953) Uprising of the Spirit (Elevación del
espíritu). 1994. Acrylic and oil on paper, Los Angeles County Museum of Art, Los Angeles,
California, U.S. © Enrique Chagoya. Used with permission of George Adams Gallery,
New York.

(though not strict dogma). So, too, with the hero myths. If we really
wish to understand them from an ancient point of view, we need to
push further into the dynamics of an alien cultural category. As we
shall see, it (unlike the modern "hero" idea) is also a religious category. Attempting a definition is worthwhile.

HERO: THE ANCIENT IDEA

What would a Greek of around 500 BC think of all this? She would,
of course, recognize our word – *hêrôs* (and its feminine equivalent
hêrôinê) remained pretty much unchanged in form, if not meaning,
as they made their way from ancient Greek into modern languages
including English. But the idea that *anyone* could be a hero would

seem terribly odd. For that matter, even the notion that a contemporary living person might be so named would strike Greeks as weird. From what we can gather, based on the evidence of archaeology and references to "heroes" in the surviving literature, this category of mortal man or woman, to the ancients, had the following characteristics.

DEAD

While it may sound harsh, this is the primary difference compared with the modern concept. *Hêrôs* was not a term of honor awarded to someone who accomplished some major deed and still lived among mortals. (On the poetry of Homer, which seems at first to contradict this, see further below.) It was a way of describing someone who had passed away and yet was remembered in quite specific ways. An anthropologist looking at Greek customs would say that the attention given to dead heroes at its core most resembles the cults of ancestors that are still prominent features of life in parts of sub-Saharan Africa and Asia. Continued veneration of ancestors affects the fortune of a household, or success in farming or hunting. Acknowledging the special skills of deceased family members through continued ritual attention (what scholars call "cult") can aid the living. Some tribespeople of central New Guinea preserve the skulls of women who were renowned in life for managing pigs, and invoke their help. In short, the dead ancestors are still a part of the family; their inability to do actual work is compensated for by their access to mysterious powers of the other world, which they can direct to the good of their descendants.

Greek hero-cult differs from generalized ancestor worship, however, in a few aspects. A given family might indeed continue the veneration of a particular ancestor – for instance, the Eumolpidae, a priestly clan at Eleusis west of Athens, which controlled the famous Mysteries there, traced its ancestry to Eumolpus "Good Singer" (i.e. of ritual chants), while his son Kêrux ("herald") gave his name to a guild of these sacred functionaries. But much more commonly, the dead heroes held an importance for wider communities, not restricted by the claims of just one clan. Theseus, for example, was venerated as the hero who helped all of Athens, as we shall in more detail below.

WORSHIPPED

This brings us to the second distinctive feature of Greek hero concepts, the idea that these celebrated persons were to be honored with religious rituals every year, at the spot where their bones lay. Special forms of sacrifice (e.g. pouring the animal's blood into the earth) marked the worship of heroes. Similarities can be detected with the later Christian cult of the saints, but the Greeks did *not* believe that heroes somehow "interceded" with the gods: instead, on their own they possessed vital powers. Their talismanic bones were thus essential acquisitions. Whichever city had them could be assured of protection against its enemies. Often in historical times, heroic bone-retrieval was coordinated by Apollo's oracle at Delphi. The travel writer Pausanias (second century AD) relates many such stories – for instance, that the bones of Arcas, son of Callisto (on whom see Chapter 2) were transferred to Mantinea in Arcadia where the locals sacrificed to him in a sacred precinct. The historian Herodotus relates an unusually detailed story (*Histories* 1.65–1.68) of how the Spartans used heroic bones to gain superiority over their enemies. The Delphic oracle assured them that removing from Tegea (also in Arcadia) the remains of Orestes, son of the Trojan War leader Agamemnon, would make the Spartans masters of the place. Guided only by an enigmatic utterance that the hero's corpse lay "where two winds blow under strong compulsion and blow lies upon blow," a Spartan named Lichas happened on a blacksmith at his forge, who revealed that he had recently discovered a gigantic skeleton in a coffin under his courtyard. The oracle's obscure reference (to bellows, hammer and anvil) now made clear, the Spartans contrived to recover what was left of Orestes, thus assuring future victories.

An even stranger story has to do with the last days of Oedipus, the notorious king of Thebes who unwittingly killed his father and married his mother. His discovery of these horrific deeds, and subsequent self-blinding, was depicted in the tragedy by Sophocles (c. 424 BC) *Oedipus the King*. Years later, exiled from his country, the aged Oedipus comes with his daughter Antigone to Athens, to a grove of the divine Furies (Erinyes). He knows that this will be his final resting place, where the presence of his numinous body will deter enemies. Cursing his former city, he calls down blessings on Theseus, the Athenian king who welcomes him. The episode was the basis of Sophocles' last play, *Oedipus at Colonus* (written about 406 BC). There seems to have been a real shrine of Oedipus in a grove in this suburb of Athens. It is not coincidental that Thebes was in the late fifth century an enemy of Athens. In sum, through myth as stylized in drama, the Athenians reassured themselves of the protective power of this immigrant hero.

But how could Oedipus, infamously entangled with incest and parricide, ever be worshiped? Folklorists have drawn attention to the career of Oedipus as embodying the motif of the Holy Sinner, the scorned but redeemed person whose experience of the depths of suffering or depravity has given him or her knowledge beyond

Figure 3.2 Oedipus, self-blinded after the discovery of his unintentional parricide and incest, departs from Thebes with his daughter Antigone, reviled by plague-stricken citizens. In Athens he later gains power to heal and to defend the community, after a mysterious death. Painting by Ernest Hillemacher (1843)

Source: AA357393 Hillemacher, Ernest (1818–1887) Oedipus, blind after plucking out his eyes, with his daughter Antigone during the plague in Thebes. Location: Musée des Beaux Arts Orléans, Photo Credit: Alfredo Dagli Orti/The Art Archive at Art Resource, NY.

the normal humans. Blind Oedipus has a second, deeper sight. Who better might be found to carry out curses than one whose own life was accursed? And who more suitably propitiated, lest his wrath turn against you? Oedipus remains in the landscape as an icon of (potentially useful) anger, like the Furies themselves. These divinities, in local Athenian belief, guaranteed fertility since, at Athena's urging, they had taken up residence under the earth and turned their vengeful anger (once directed at the kin-killer Orestes) against any sort of threats to their newly adopted city, its people and crops. (That story is dramatized in the *Furies* by Aeschylus, part of the *Oresteia* tragic trilogy of 458 BC.)

LOCALIZED

Because heroes are associated with their graves, they are inherently local. In fact, the hero myths by starting out as "epichoric" narratives provided a constant and contrary tug against the "Panhellenic" tendencies of myths about gods. The pantheon of the divine settled down, throughout Greek lands, to a generally agreed-on number of twelve: Zeus, Hera, and the other Olympians (with minor local variations). But there were some 900 or so heroes – and those are just the ones whose names we find attested in later literature or inscriptions. Some are mere names to us, since their mythic tales were never transmitted. We would love to know the backstory for figures like the hero *Akratopotês* (Drinker of Unmixed Wine), honored at Mounichia near the Athenian port, of the Spartan heroes *Mattôn* (Kneader) and *Keraôn* (Mixer), not to mention the hero of Achaea named *Deipneus* (from *deipna* "dinners"), who were alluded to by the second-century AD writer Athenaeus (*Deipnosophistae* 1.39c–39d). At any rate, it is far from accidental that the number of heroes in the landscape, many of them only names, corresponds well with the number of city-states for which we have evidence in the archaic and classical periods of Greece – approximately 800, some of them the size of small towns. Every *polis* could lay claim to its heroes and heroines. Sometimes these would be founding figures, and their grave would be located in the *agora* or public center of the settlement. Others are given random reasons for ending up in a specific locale: Pausanias, the travel writer, observed the grave of Penelope, the wife of Odysseus, in Tegea in Arcadia. She died there some years after retiring to her father's Spartan home (so the local story went) because Odysseus had accused her of having sex with her suitors during his extended struggle to return to Ithaca.

SOMETIMES BEHAVE BADLY

A person gifted with powers above the norm – physical strength, cunning, or simply a much larger capacity for strong emotions – is both beneficial and dangerous. It depends on how the powers are directed and controlled. The single most disturbing difference between our use of "hero" and the ancient concept is that the latter did *not* imply morally upright behavior. (Of course, one could argue that modern celebrities, whether TV reality show stars, athletes or drug lords are heroized without regard to morals.) Shocked as we may be to hear of the hero-cult accorded Oedipus, it is perhaps odder to hear myths in which the main character clearly does something wrong and yet rather than being punished gains status as a hero or heroine.

Take the following two examples.

Kleomedes, from the island Astypalaia, was a boxer living in historical times – a figure of legend, rather than myth. He forfeited his victory at the Olympic Games in 492 BC because he ended up killing his opponent. Back home, his resentment at this loss brought on a fit of madness, in which he knocked over the supporting pillars of a school house and killed sixty children. Pursued by the angry islanders, he took refuge in a chest inside the temple of Athena. When this was pried open and found to be empty the astounded Astypalaians sent to the Delphic oracle to clear up the mystery. In reply they were told to "Honor Kleomedes with sacrifices, the last of the Heroes, no longer mortal" – which they did, from then on. Not only does this anecdote remind us that heroization was an ongoing process in antiquity, applied, albeit rarely, to important political figures or warriors (such as the Spartan general Brasidas, killed in 422 BC during the war with Athens). It also indicates that the "accomplishment" of the heroized individual could simply be something so uncanny or unbelievable that its memory would never fade.

The second example is Medea. The heroine of a tragedy by Euripides (produced in 431 BC) – in the literary sense of its main fictional character – she seems to have been in real life an object of devotion associated with the worship of Hera in Corinth. That goddess was originally responsible for making Medea fall in love with Jason when he visited her far eastern home, Colchis, in search of the Golden Fleece. After helping him win it and escape, Medea bore him two sons, but later murdered them in an act of revenge when Jason took a new bride. (Other versions of the myth say that the Corinthians themselves committed the crime and blamed her, or that Medea accidentally killed her offspring trying to immortalize them.) At the end of Euripides' drama, Medea promises to establish a hero-cult to her dead children, in the precinct of Hera *Akraia*, near Corinth. She then flees the scene – scot-free – on a snake-drawn chariot belonging to her grandfather, the sun god Helios. To top off this chilling tale, yet other versions claimed that an immortalized Medea joined Achilles as his bride in the Elysian Fields, after his death. As we shall see, Medea's career moves are more transgressive than those of the usual Greek heroine. From another viewpoint, however, she is simply the quintessence of the tendency to challenge norms and cross boundary-lines that characterizes all heroic figures, women or men.

HEROES IN HOMER AND HESIOD

The defining traits and mythic stories mentioned so far might seem unusual to those who read the great epics attributed to the poet Homer (c. 700 BC). In the *Iliad* and the *Odyssey*, the word *hêrôs* (occurring about 100 times, in total) is regularly used for living warriors whose mighty deeds are described blow-for-blow, sometimes *en masse* ("the Achaean heroes"), sometimes as individuals, both Greek and Trojan (Agamemnon, the doctor-warrior Machaon, et al.). Only two so designated are actually dead, in the chronological terms of the poem itself – Laomedon, a past king at Troy, and Protesilaos, the first Greek fighter to lose his life there. In the *Odyssey*, the word has even more tenuous connections to the themes of martial valor and death: Telemachus, the twenty-something son of Odysseus, who has never been to battle, and Demodokos, the palace bard of the mythical Phaeacian islanders, are both called *hêrôs*, as if the word is being used honorifically, something like "the noble person X."

Did the concept change from the time of Homer? Or is something more complex at work? As it turns out, the poems attributed to Hesiod, which were discussed in Chapter 2, are of exactly the same vintage as Homeric epic, but provide a different picture. We cannot therefore argue for evolution or progressive reinterpretation. In Hesiod's description of the Five Ages, Zeus makes a fourth generation "a godlike race of hero-men who are called demi-gods, the race before our own." The poet specifies the two major wars in which these heroes were involved: at Thebes (after the death of Oedipus and the ensuing clash between his sons) and at Troy. Some died, says the poet, but the others:

> Zeus sent to dwell at the edges of earth, and they live untouched by sorrow in the islands of the blessed along the shore of deep swirling Ocean, happy heroes for whom the grain-giving earth bears honey-sweet fruit flourishing thrice a year, far from the deathless gods.
>
> (Trans. H. Evelyn-White)

This vision of heroic immortality in the Isles of the Blessed (a multiform of the Elysian Fields) freely admits what Homeric epic allows us to have only the faintest suspicion about – that heroes continue to live after death. In sum, for the full picture of the epic *hêrôs*, we need to use binocular vision, taking into account both Homer and Hesiod: heroes die but they also "live" again.

This ideology must be what the Greeks had in mind when they worshiped at the tombs of those whom they identified as figures from the Homeric poems. Prime among them was Achilles, the greatest Greek warrior at Troy, who had a hero-cult at Leuke in the Black Sea and Olbia (in what is now Ukraine), as well as several parts of Greece (Epirus, Thessaly, Elis). In the lattermost, we are told by Pausanias (6.23.3), an empty tomb of Achilles was the site each year of ceremonies in honor of the hero, with the local women engaging in lamentation. That Achilles had this cenotaph in Elis, but annual rites as in hero-cults at actual tombs, fits with the notion that he is "really" not dead but living in a distant happy place. (Urban legends to the same effect have been told of Elvis, FDR, and other modern celebrities.) When we come to the myths of Heracles, the same split-screen mentality will emerge: just as heroes are half-mortal and semi-divine, so they must be dead while not-dead (since they are powerful after death as healers, cursers and protectors). Another way of looking at this unusual phenomenon – one that makes the ancient reception of Homer very different from our own – is that the audience for the *Iliad* and *Odyssey* could feel closer to the characters of the poems because these still existed in their own landscapes (or at least they knew of them being worshiped somewhere in Greece).

Archaeology bears out what we learn from ancient literary sources. In Mycenae, the legendary home of Agamemnon, who led the Trojan expedition to retrieve his abducted sister-in-law Helen, archaic graffiti show that local people had set up a shrine to the hero. If the approximate date of the Trojan War is 1200 BC (on the basis of ancient reckoning as well as modern archaeological discoveries at Troy's probable location), then Agamemnon was still being commemorated in his home territory some 500 years later. Of course, Homeric poetry itself, crystallizing in its present form centuries after the supposed siege of Troy, would help sustain the memory. At Therapne, three miles south of Sparta, a shrine for Agamemnon's brother Menelaus and for Helen, where they were said to be buried, was founded sometime before 700 BC. As with a number of other similar shrines, the anonymous worshipers located their sanctuary above Mycenaean remains – that is to say, at a settlement that actually dated back to the time of the epic heroes. Mycenaean civilization, the earliest detectable phase of Greek culture, lasted from about 1600 to 1150 BC, and may have declined precisely because its local kings overextended their manpower and resources in expeditions like the one to Troy. It has been suggested that the people of a later era believed the old tombs contained heroic figures from this earlier, mightier time, and so treated them as heroes.

Most intriguing are the twelve bronze tripods found in Polis Cave on Ithaca, a spot we know saw dedications to Odysseus well into historical times. Strikingly, in the *Odyssey*, we see the hero store tripods given him by the Phaeacians in an Ithacan cave upon his return. But archaeologists date these particular large three-legged ceremonial basins to the ninth and eighth centuries BC – well before the Homeric epics had been diffused throughout Greek lands. It is possible, therefore, that Odysseus was already being celebrated as a non-epic local hero, with contests and tripod-dedications on Ithaca, before the poems ever came to celebrate him. In the later generations when the Homeric poems began to be elaborated, the reputation of a powerful king who once ruled over a western island would have ensured that Odysseus gained a foothold in this new Panhellenic medium. While the local hero-cult of Odysseus probably preceded his appearance in poetry, once epic became popular the two institutions – cult and poetry – became mutually supportive. The latter gives a vivid imaginative backstory to the ongoing ceremonies of the former.

HEROINES

To speak of Greek hero myths is to tell only half the story. One might think, from the way they were represented in art and literature, that ancient Greek men (like others in some traditional societies even to this day), were war-oriented, patriarchal, and misogynistic. The myth of Pandora, the fabricated woman who brought countless ills to mortals, seems to encapsulate a bleak male view of women (see Chapter 2). Satirical poetry offers a similar take. Consider, for example, the poem by Semonides of Amorgos (seventh century BC) which systematically catalogues different types of women in terms of their alleged resemblance to dogs, vixens, horses, donkeys, weasels, or bees (the most desirable). A welcome wave of feminist scholarship in Classics starting in the late 1960s to some extent overplayed this caricature of Greek macho culture. At the same time, it helpfully increased our appreciation for the many ways in which Greek myth actually confirms a very different view of women – as powerful, clever, and enduring (albeit at times unpredictable and dangerous). This can be seen not just in stories of cunning goddesses like Athena and Aphrodite, Circe and Calypso, who manipulate and even ruin mortals. More surprisingly, the positive message about women is relayed in a number of tales of mortal women who gained significant cultural importance. There were a number of routes to becoming a heroine in the ancient Greek imagination. We'll focus on two.

First, a woman might be celebrated for having lived, and be worshiped after her death with annual rites, because she was related to a hero (often having similar honors) either as sister, daughter, wife, or mother. While this might seem to cast women in a distinctly secondary role, such connections are actually a sign of recognition that the female environment of the house, and a male's earliest habituation, do play an outsized role in his later development. Some of these women exist only as names attached to better-known males. In Argos, (east-central Greece), Kerdô ("Gain") had a shrine in the city-state's *agora*. She was known simply as the wife of Phoroneus, a primeval culture-hero of the region who was honored for having introduced the worship of Hera and the use of fire (like a homegrown Prometheus). Perhaps Kerdô's name expressed the useful advantages brought by her husband: about her, specifically, nothing more is transmitted. Of the more than 400 heroines for whom some form of worship is attested in Greece, and of whom we know some more details, a large number can be attached to celebrity males: Alcmene, for example (mother of Heracles); Callisto (mother by Zeus of Arkas founder of Arcadia); Gorgophonê (daughter of Perseus); Hygieia ("Health," daughter of the doctor-hero Asclepius); Penelope (wife of Odysseus and, by some scandalous accounts, mother of the god Pan by her suitors). In the religious and athletic center of Olympia it was said that the bones of Hippodameia were buried. She was known as the wife for whom the hero Pelops (who gave his name to the Peloponnese) risked and won a life-threatening bride-contest, in which the potential father-in-law used to pursue suitors by chariot to kill them. Later banished by Pelops (she allegedly let their son Chrysippos be killed), after her death Hippodameia's bones were sent back to Olympia at the command of an oracle. Annually the women of the city honored this "heroine" with sacrifices. Although their individual stories often remain unheard in the literary sources, no doubt the women of the localities where she was buried had rich traditions of tales, songs, and material crafts that commemorated their heroine. From the practices of women nowadays in traditional cultures, such as India, we can infer the central role that local (even secret) rituals and art-forms played in keeping memories of ancestral "heroines" alive.

A more extensive version of the family-connected heroine can be seen in the tale of Semele. This mortal woman was a daughter of Cadmus, the wandering hero who founded Thebes in Boeotia while searching for his sister Europe (abducted from Phoenicia by Zeus and herself later worshiped in Crete). Semele, too, became pregnant by Zeus; his jealous wife Hera persuaded her to beg her divine lover to appear in his actual form. This, unfortunately, turned out to be that of a thunderbolt. Zeus took their unborn child from the womb of his incinerated beloved and after sewing him into his thigh, "bore" the god Dionysos when the baby had reached full term.

No special deed, other than that of being one of Zeus's many conquests, marks Semele. Yet, for bearing the god she herself passes into immortality. Though dead (like all other mortal heroines) she is also "alive" under the name of "Thyone." One version has her son Dionysos recovering Semele from Hades, dank abode of all who have passed away. Within the sanctuary of Dionysos in Thebes, the spot where Semele died was highly venerated. So, too, were the several places identified with her "resurrection" from the underworld At Delphi, a festival called *Heroïs* was devoted to the return of the heroine; its rites were known only to the "thuiads" or worshipers of Dionysos. In Erchia, a rural district near Athens, Semele and her son each received a goat as sacrificial offering shortly after each year's Dionysia festival in the city. From this and other evidence about her, it is plausible that Semele was tied into fertility rituals and the yearly flourishing of vegetation – not unlike Persephone, daughter of Demeter, who was abducted to be bride of Hades. To a greater extent than happens with hero myths, those of heroines can tend to overlap with narratives of goddesses.

The first category, heroines-by-association, stands in contrast to a second in which the women involved take on more active roles. Still, the extended family seems to be at the core of their stories. A series of heroines were celebrated for having sacrificed themselves at moments of crisis, thus saving their immediate kin and the people of their country. After Heracles died, his overbearing cousin Eurystheus, who had overseen the hero's twelve labors in life, persecuted the hero's children. An Athenian king (a son of Theseus) undertook to defend them, but discovered from an oracle that only the sacrifice of a well-born maiden would give his army victory. Macaria, the daughter of Heracles, volunteered to die. The moving story formed the basis of *The Children of Heracles*, a drama by Euripides (produced c. 430 BC). Given this mythic resonance, the title *Macaria, or Altars of Sacrifice* was aptly chosen by the Southern writer Augusta Jane Evans for her best-selling 1864 novel about the self-sacrificing efforts of women in the Confederate States.

A variant on this motif has a set of heroic sisters dying for a greater cause. At Athens, the Hyacinthidae were honored each year by dancing choruses of young women. The mythical Athenian king Erechtheus (later heroized and worshiped on the Acropolis) was in many traditions their father. Once again, voluntary sacrifice by one

or all of the girls led to military victory – this time, over the people of Eleusis near Athens, under the command of Poseidon's son
Eumolpus (the "Good Singer" whom we mentioned above, heroized
in turn by people of *his* locality). Euripides wrote a tragedy on this
episode, as well (*Erechtheus*, c. 422–412 BC), of which only fragments
survive from the ancient script.

A third story of this type that fascinated Euripides was about
Iphigenia, daughter of Agamemnon. The Athenian tragic playwright
wrote two dramas concerning her heroine myth, *Iphigenia at Aulis*,
written between 408 and 406 BC, and *Iphigenia in Tauris*, written
between 416 BC and 412 BC. Agamemnon, leader of the expedition
to Troy, did not properly honor Artemis. In anger, the goddess of
the hunt stops the winds that would have propelled his fleet from
Aulis, and will not be satisfied until the commander sacrifices his
eldest daughter. Iphigenia is lured to Troy under the false pretext that
she will get to marry the stupendous warrior Achilles. Even when
the cynical lie is revealed, she willingly offers herself for sacrifice.
In this Euripidean version, however (unlike that told by the older
playwright Aeschylus a half-century earlier), Iphigenia disappears
from the altar. It emerges that the goddess Artemis had replaced her
would-be victim on the altar with a fawn at the last moment, instead
taking the girl to Tauris (now Crimea). There she stays for the dura-
tion of the Trojan War, presiding as priestess of her savior's temple,
but with the awful task of killing any Greeks who approach it.

As luck would have it, her own brother Orestes, who killed
his mother Clytemnestra in revenge for murdering his father
Agamemnon when he returned victorious from Troy, visits the
shrine of Artemis. He has been sent by Apollo in order to rid himself of the Furies (Erinyes) that still haunt him for the matricide. In
typical Euripidean fashion, tragedy is averted in the nick of time:
Iphigenia is led to recognize her brother, and the pair flee with a
stolen talismanic statue of Artemis. It is subsequently brought to a
new temple of the goddess, in Brauron east of Athens (see Chapter 2
on girls' rituals there).

Iphigenia's sacrificial death and the compensation for it are commemorated, as with Semele, by the dual existence of worship at her
"tomb" (in Megara, southwest of Athens, according to Pausanias
1.43.1) and devotion paid to her as an immortal goddess named
"Artemis of the Road" (*Einodia*) or *Orsilochia* (a name associated

with pangs of childbirth). That this status of cult-heroine might be even older than the period of the Trojan War is suggested by an intriguing reference to sacrifices intended for one "Iphimedea" on a Mycenaean-period "Linear B" tablet from the western Greek region of Pylos (PY 172). As with Medea (see above), another version has Iphigenia married after death to Achilles, this time in Leuke, the "White Island" (another multiform of the paradisal Elysian Fields) where he spends his post-mortem time.

We come finally to perhaps the best-known of Greek sacrificial heroines, Antigone. Her name has been interpreted to mean "against" or "in exchange for" or "equal to" (*anti*) "generation" (*gon-ê* – the same root as "genesis"). The slightly varied meanings encapsulate the paradox of her mythic story: glory for herself because she has suffered for the family, but a personal failure to produce offspring, since she dies before consummating her marriage. Like the basic pattern seen in the Iphigenia myth, this narrative revolves around a compensation – her life in exchange for a higher ideal. Unlike the other heroine stories, there is hardly any evidence for this tale before the tragic drama produced by Sophocles (perhaps c. 440 BC). It could be that Sophocles invented the story, embedding deep mythic themes. As we have pointed out in the previous chapter, such creativity and innovation within a body of accepted myths is in fact traditional – we simply don't get the chance to observe it up close so dramatically, as most myths come down to us under the guise of age-old lore anonymously transmitted.

Antigone is the daughter of the ill-fated Oedipus by his wife (also, mother) Jocasta. Even before her father's death in exile, her brothers Eteocles and Polynices have started a deadly quarrel over inheritance back at their native city, Thebes. In the ensuing war, Polynices is killed. The tyrannical ruler of Thebes, Creon, prohibits burial for this rebellious brother, leaving his corpse to rot uncovered. Antigone risks arrest by caring for it, putting the unwritten law of the gods above the human pronouncement of Creon. She is sentenced to death by being placed in an underground tomb, alive, where she then hangs herself. Creon's son, her fiancé Haemon, commits suicide next to her body. In the brilliant Sophoclean dramatic rendition, questions about the very basis of society clash on stage: where does loyalty lie, with the city-state or the extended family (living and dead)? Which is better, (male) rationality, wanting to control earth, nature, and people?

Or (female) emotionality, able to integrate itself with nature? The Classicist Charles Segal has pointed out that, over and above these binary oppositions, *Antigone* stages a contest between *logos* (reasoned thinking, straightforward verbal accounting) and *mythos* (the sort of verbal artistry where ambiguous and multiple meanings predominate). In other words, *Antigone* – the heroine "myth" that may be mostly pure fifth-century invention – reaches the essential workings of "myth" at the deepest level.

The popularity of the story and drama has increased with every world conflict, it seems. Its "reception history" (something we'll study more in Chapter 5) includes a version by the French dramatist Jean Anouilh (1910–87), produced in 1944 in Nazi-occupied Paris, and four years later, a version by the German playwright Bertolt Brecht, based on an early nineteenth-century translation by Hölderlin, but costumed as if during World War II. In 1970s South Africa, *The Island*, by Athol Fugard, dramatized the bleak existence of political prisoners under the apartheid regime, two of whom keep their sanity by rehearsing in their cell a performance of the *Antigone*, one playing the heroine and the other Creon. In 1984, the Irish playwright Aidan Carl Mathews set the plot in an Orwellian dystopia with allusions to the troubles in Northern Ireland, while another Irishman, Tom Paulin, produced *The Riot Act*, based on the Sophocles play. Recent years have seen the *Antigone Project* (a response to the constraints of the US Patriot Act); a 2014 performance by Syrian refugee women in Beirut; and Femi Osofisan's 1999 version, *Tegonni: An African Antigone*, a meditation on colonialism in his native Nigeria. Remarkably a play more nearly 2,500 years old, rooted in even older mythic templates of the heroine, remains the most adaptable and politically charged of Greek dramas.

HEROIC QUESTS AND THEIR MEANING

The religious figures at the heart of the stories of heroes and heroines, as we have seen, generate certain kinds of narratives that necessarily focus on the power but also death and afterlife of the protagonist. The distinctions between male and female strains of the heroic have to do with their complementary relationships to the community, which might be described as *internal* (centered on family, kin obligations, reproduction – e.g. Medea, Semele, and Antigone) as contrasted with *external* (male defense of the community against outside forces – the saga-cycles focused on Thebes and Troy). We might expand the latter variety to include those especially popular narratives in which a young male goes on a quest that ultimately benefits either his family or community. Such myths have, additionally, attracted the attention of modern folklorists and narratologists – professional analysts of how stories get transmitted and are structured. The heroes Perseus and Jason will serve to illustrate a shared typology.

Perseus (the name means "Destroyer") was not supposed to have been born. His grandfather, Acrisius, was told by an oracle that a son of his daughter would eventually kill him, so he placed the girl (Danaë) in a bronze underground vault (one recalls Antigone's end). Zeus, however, in the form of a golden stream managed to seep through its roof and into Danaë's lap, impregnating her. Acrisius, all the more terrified, sealed Danaë in a chest with her baby and set it adrift on the sea. It washed ashore on an island (Seriphos) where the boy was rescued and raised by its finder, and his mother became the object of the local king's lust. Perseus, grown to be a young man, after some unfortunate boasting was sent to bring back the head of the mythical monster, the Gorgon (a means of getting him out of the king's way). Hermes and Athena helped him; he forced three crone-like daughters of Phorcus to tell him how to find the next set of helpers, the nymphs (by withholding their sole shared tooth and eye); the nymphs, in turn, provided him with winged sandals, the *kibisis* (a special sack), and a cap of invisibility. With an adamantine sickle presented by Hermes, he decapitated Medusa, the only mortal Gorgon. In order not to be turned to stone by her fatal gaze, Perseus carried out the deed by viewing her reflection in his bronze shield, then fled with the head in his protective *kibisis*. But the adventure is only half over.

Even in summary, the reader can tell that the pleasure of this myth derives from its folktale motifs and repetitions – three sets of three sisters, doubled helpers, magic objects and monsters living beyond the real world. At the same time, however, it resembles other Greek myths in being mostly grounded on a specific geography (the real island Seriphos) and deep-seated, sociopolitical problems (e.g. overthrow by descendants – as in the *Theogony* myths).

Perseus returned to the real world at what Greeks considered one of its edges, Ethiopia. There he discovered that a sea-monster was about to devour Andromeda, daughter of the king Cepheus. Cepheus' wife's unseemly boasting (another repeated motif) had angered Poseidon and the sea nymphs, who sent a flood and monster toward his land. Only the sacrifice of Andromeda (chained to a rock by the sea) would avert the catastrophe. (Note the sacrificial-maiden plot as in heroine tales.) Promised the girl as wife if he can slay the monster, Perseus did so, dispatched a rival lover by confronting him with Medusa's petrifying head, returned to Seriphos and did the same to the bad suitor-king and his henchmen, thus saving Danaë, his mother. Athena, his divine guide, placed the Gorgon's head at the center of her shield.

It does not take much inventiveness to read this myth as pre-pubescent fantasy. Psychoanalyst critics have delighted in explicating its images of monster-slaying and decapitation (yet another doubling in the plot), along with the treatment of women (on which more below). Oedipal themes are not far off, either. Just as the Theban hero unwittingly killed his father Laius, so Perseus ends up accidentally striking his grandfather Acrisius with a discus while competing in a pentathlon after his adventures. Once more, he is forced to leave Argos, the land of his birth.

The Perseus myth segues by way of genealogical links into the grand cycle of Heracles myths, that we shall turn to shortly. At this point however, it is worthwhile comparing another popular quest myth, the story of Jason and the Argonauts. The hero (whose name means "Healer") comes from further north, the city of Iolcus (now Volos) on the Gulf of Pagasae. Like Perseus, he is embroiled unwillingly in political questions of royal succession. His father Aeson was half-brother of Pelias, the ruler of Iolcus, who was warned by an oracle that a man with one sandal would threaten his kingdom. Jason arrives for a sacrifice after losing one sandal in a river, so Pelias sends him on an impossible mission, to retrieve the Golden Fleece, a sheepskin that (for other complicated reasons) hangs in a grove in Colchis on the Black Sea (modern-day Georgia), where an unsleeping dragon protects it. As with Perseus, Athena provides help for the quest. Jason builds the ship *Argo* (according to some, the very first naval vessel) and assembles a crack team of the finest heroes, including Castor and Pollux, Peleus (eventual father of Achilles), Laertes (who will beget Odysseus), Heracles, the singer Orpheus, and another two dozen or so men. In effect, this is the roster of star heroes in the generation immediately before that of the Trojan War. Unlike the story of Perseus's lone quest, the tale of the Argonauts ("sailors on the *Argo*") acknowledges the collective action by a group of young men who are separated from kin, encounter challenges together, and return safely home. It thus resembles another celebrated major Greek collective adventure, the boar hunt at Calydon, as well as the massive Panhellenic action of the Troy saga. (The *Odyssey*, as well, begins with a sort of miniature collective quest, as Telemachus son of Odysseus gathers a crew of men his age to sail for word of his missing father.) From the point of view of social institutions, it is likely that the story about Jason and the Argonauts embodies ideals and models good for narrating in the context of young male initiation rites.

Even more than the Perseus myth, that of the Argonauts has been elaborated by repetitions and exciting digressive episodes, from night battles with allies mistaken for enemies, to encounters with the monstrous winged Harpies. The longest extant continuous version is the elegant epic *Argonautica* by Apollonius of Rhodes, a scholar-poet working in the Greek cosmopolitan center Alexandria in Egypt during the first half of the third century BC. Because Apollonius had completely absorbed the Homeric *Odyssey* and *Iliad* (at that time being edited and intensively studied in his city) many of the episodes of his own poem, like that of the Clashing Rocks, Sirens, and Scylla and Charybdis, are meant to echo specific epic predecessors in the mind of his sophisticated urban audience. In other words, we cannot disentangle the bare-bones plot of the tale from later poetic additions. Then again, as we have seen, the growth of mythic narratives inevitably involves performance and innovation such as that by Apollonius: just because we cannot view the process in a pre-literary world does not mean that oral storytellers of the older tale had not already contributed elaborations and backstory material. Scholars suspect that a version of the Argonaut story was already available to the poet of the archaic *Odyssey*, so that Apollonius' older model was itself shaped on a replay of the quest. And in fact, the *Odyssey* in a reference to the Clashing Rocks (*Od.* 12.78–80) explicitly alludes to a pre-existing story of "the *Argo*, which all people care about."

We have already mentioned the culmination of this story – the love of Medea, daughter of the Colchian king, for Jason and her aid in stealing the Fleece. Apollonius beautifully teases out the maiden's

psychological state, through speech and simile, while not neglect-
ing the rousing action-hero elements of the scenario (fire-breathing
bulls, magic protective ointment, an army of skeletal men who
spring up from dragon's teeth). No wonder that the renowned
Ray Harryhausen (1920–2013) saw in this epic an opportunity to
deploy his innovative stop-motion special effects, when he collabo-
rated with Don Chaffey (1917–90) on the now classic *Jason and the
Argonauts* (1963). Apart from such surface spectacles, however, the
Argonaut saga offers, like the Perseus story, an interesting pattern
when it comes to relations with women and kin. Perseus, as we
have seen, kills one female (the Gorgon Medusa) and wins another
(Andromeda); the causal link between deed and reward is empha-
sized by the detail of his using the snaky-haired head of Medusa to
incapacitate his rival for marriage. His success ultimately frees from
anxiety yet another woman, his mother Danaë.

With Jason, on the other hand, sex comes first in the narrative
sequence. He and his crew land early on at the island of Lemnos,
where a bizarre series of events has led to a population comprising
only love-starved women and their children (the Lemnian women
having killed their husbands and fathers). Mass coupling ensues.
Jason takes the queen Hypsipyle to bed, creating sons who will later
help the Trojan War effort. Jason's quest involves killing a monster,
but unlike Medusa this is not marked as female; the reward for the
deed is also his helper in doing it (Medea – not Athena, as in the
Perseus tale); and upon his return to Greece, there is no mother to be
rescued, only a deceased father to be avenged. Medea helps here, as
well, by persuading the daughters of the bad king Pelias to chop him
up and boil him. As she demonstrates on a sacrificial ram, she possesses sorceress powers that can rejuvenate any slaughtered creature.
Of course, she does not end up reviving Pelias. In hindsight, given
this tale, Medea's infanticide at Corinth (see above) might have been
predicted, especially since she had already on the flight from Colchis
chopped up and dumped overboard her own brother in order to
distract her pursuers.

How do we deal with these seemingly kaleidoscopic patterns,
sometimes forming resemblances, at other times bright contrasts?
Even onomastics seems to hint at some deeper bonds, as if the tales
form portions of a larger submerged template. The names Medea,
Medusa, and Andromeda all share a verbal root *med-*, which

goes back to Greek's parent language and culture, Indo-European. Linguists reconstruct for this root an original meaning "take appropriate measures." It underlies words for skilled professions in the various daughter languages – in Latin *medicus* (doctor) and in Old Irish *midiur* (I judge). Other Greek mythic figures have it as well: Clytai-m(n)estra (cunning wife of Agamemnon, whose name means "Famous for Devising") and Mêtis (Cunning Intelligence), the wife of Zeus who produces (through her husband's head) the ultimate goddess of measured skill – Athena. Without reducing the diverting variations in the complementary tales of Jason and Perseus to an algebraic abstraction, we can nevertheless suggest that both myths delineate the advantages and dangers of female intelligence for a maturing male. On the dangerous end of the spectrum is Medusa, who paralyzes her victims with a stony stare; on the positive, helpful end is Andromeda, the princess-bride (note: *herself* immobilized *by* men, when Perseus first encounters her chained to a rock); in between – and therefore the most tricky to deal with – is Medea, helpful wife but ultimately nightmarish monster-mother. It is as if the message to young men who would have been told these tales is: be aware of the possibilities of a completely alien creature, Woman. This, of course, is in very different language and images, simply a replay of one underlying lesson of the creation stories that we analyzed in Chapter 2. Pandora, the beautiful evil, is mythic prototype of all later "designing women."

HERO PATTERNS

Precisely such parallels and overlaps have caught the attention of those looking for some deeper organizing principle beneath the otherwise multifarious quest tales of heroes. It is worthwhile examining two influential attempts at uncovering basic patterns. Some further attempts, specifically tied to depth psychology, will be discussed in the next chapter, when we turn to modern interpreters of myths.

Vladimir Propp (1895–1970) was one of the first modern scholars to try to articulate the core structures of popular tales – in his case, not Greek myths but Russian "wonder-tales," more akin to folk- and fairy-stories. In his *Morphology of the Folktale* (Russian edition 1928; English translation 1958) Propp mined a database of hundreds of such tales and proposed that the characters in them could be reduced to a mere seven key spheres of action (or "actants"): Villain, Hero, Dispatcher, Magic Helper, Princess and her Father, Donor, and False Hero. We can extrapolate from Propp to confirm that this basic kit helps in constructing Greek hero myths, as well – at least to some extent. In the Perseus and Jason stories, notice that some of these roles merge, while others are absent (significantly, there are no "false heroes" who claim to be the real one). The Dispatcher of the Hero on the dangerous quest is also the Villain (Pelias, or the king of Seriphos); but monsters can also be villains (Medusa, the sea monster); the gods or nymphs play the role of Magic Helpers or Donors (but so does Medea); as we observed already, in the Argonaut story the Princess and the Helper (and Donor) are identical. In short, Propp's roles can be detected but the deeper interest of the myths arises because they do *not* play out the same predictable series of actants in exactly the same way. In addition, Propp theorized that wonder-tales (again, not necessarily myths) were built on thirty-one "functions" or plot-events, always in the same sequence, although some might be omitted. These include "absentation" (the hero leaves his home); an interdiction and its violation (a character does what he has been told to avoid); illustration of the villain's trickery and its harmful results; receipt of a magical agent, struggle, victory, pursuit, and return home. Once more, we can easily identify these in the Greek quest stories, but what becomes more interesting is the way in which the Greek narratives omit or downplay certain functions – in particular, it is as though the villains in Greek myth are deprived of agency. The kings who send Perseus and Jason to almost certain death don't spend time reconnoitering ahead of time or interrupting the hero's journey. Medusa and the sea-monster are quite passive. There are no scenes of exposure of the villain, although Propp's functions of transfiguration for the hero and final wedding do occur. In the Jason story, however, the wedding to Medea occurs in the middle while the finale is an anti-marriage, Medea's infanticide and flight (only to wed another man elsewhere, Aegeus of Athens).

Propp is usually considered one of the Russian Formalist literary critics, but his work had an important influence on later analysts working with Structuralist techniques (on which see the Chapter 4). A second analyst writing around the same period was more of an amateur, but in some ways more noticed as he included myths from around the world in his proposed hero-tale template. FitzRoy Richard Somerset (1885–1964), the fourth Baron Raglan, was a retired British army major, gentleman farmer, and amateur scholar, especially interested in anthropology and archaeology. His 1936 volume, *The Hero*, attempted to articulate a master-plot with twenty-two features, on the basis of several dozen prominent stories. Paraphrasing Raglan, the archetypal hero: has a mother who is a royal virgin and father who is a king; has a conception or birth that are unusual (often raising suspicions of divine parentage); an attempt is made to kill him at birth, but he is spirited far away, and reared by foster parents. On reaching manhood he goes to his future kingdom; after a victory over the king and/or beast he marries a princess, often the daughter of his predecessor, and becomes king. After ruling uneventfully he loses favor with the gods and/or his subjects, is driven from the city, and meets with a mysterious death (often at the top of a hill). His children do not succeed him, his body is not buried, but he nevertheless obtains at least one holy precinct.

Clearly, Perseus fits this mold pretty well; Jason, to a lesser extent. Of the Greek heroes, Oedipus seems to meet the requirements most completely (including his mysterious death at Colonus – a name that means "hill"!), and Heracles comes a close second (without the fosterage motif). More broadly, the Irish hero Cú Chulainn, the English folk hero Robin Hood, Moses, Cyrus of Persia, and King Arthur all score high on the checklist. (Although Raglan did not dwell on it, so does Jesus Christ.) Unlike Propp, Raglan sought to find an origin for this universal patterning, coming up with the notion of a primeval ritual drama about kingship. In this he followed in the footsteps of J. G. Frazer, whose book *The Golden Bough* was basic to what became known as the "myth and ritual" school of interpretation. Both authors share, with many other late-nineteenth-century mythologists, the assumption that myth is essentially the residue of history, whether in the form of traditions about person and peoples, or long-forgotten customs. Whatever its deep structural resemblances, however, the Greek hero tales – as interpreters more recently have realized – do their work through their surfaces, the explicit connections that they make with politics and genealogy, subjects of prime importance to Greeks.

HERACLES

The career of the most famous Greek hero features not only the apparently universal patterns investigated by Raglan and Propp, but also specific Greek traits that make his story distinctive. Of particular interest is the way in which Heracles was integrated into Greek mythic history (or "mythistory," to use a helpful eighteenth-century coinage). Heracles' birth was delayed by the machinations of a jealous Hera so that his cousin Eurystheus gained sovereignty in fulfillment of an oracle that declared whoever was born on a certain day would rule. An attempt to kill Heracles when he was eight months old was made when two serpents were let into his nursery, either by Hera or his own father, who wanted to determine which of the twins born to his wife was really the god's child and which the mortal Amphitryon's. The baby Heracles' strangling of the snakes left no question.

As for exile and fosterage, the Greek myth creatively applies the theme to Heracles' father, in an attempt to account for geopolitical realities. It is a complex dynastic web, but some sense of it is necessary for appreciating the comprehensive ambitions of the Heracles saga. These go far beyond an untethered folkloric entertainment and try instead to explain why certain families rule specific places.

We start with Electryon, the son of Perseus and Andromeda. Among his brothers were Mestor, Sthenelus, and Alcaeus. Already, this lineage (through Perseus' grandfather Acrisius) connects Electryon somewhat distantly with the royal families of Thebes and Crete. That looks like a plausible historical remembrance, since Mycenae, over which Elektryon ruled, just like the other regions, was a venerable cultural center with Greek foundations reaching back to the second millennium. Electryon married the daughter of his brother Alcaeus (a common pattern in actual Greek usage), and fathered Alcmene. Alcaeus, meanwhile, fathered Amphitryon. These two cousins, in turn, married and produced Heracles and his mortal twin Iphicles (in the circumstances already mentioned above).

Now we plunge into regional politics and dynastic struggles. The story of Perseus explains, through the story of a land swap, why he and his descendants, originally from Argos in the eastern part of the Peloponnese, came to rule over Tiryns, an imposing old city about ten kilometers to the southeast of Argos, which was closely associated with Mycenae. A failed territorial deal disrupted this scene. Mestor, brother of Elektryon, had married a daughter of Pelops, ruler of the western Peloponnese region around Olympia. His grandsons, and their Taphian tribe, were further tied to north-western Greece and offshore islands such as Ithaca. When they came east to claim their grandfather's inheritance in Mycenae, Electryon refused, so they stole his cattle. Amphitryon (nephew of Elektryon) retrieved them (for which his uncle promised him Alcmene as bride). But while the cows were being put back in their pens, in a freak accident the club Amphitryon was using to herd them struck and killed his uncle (a familial motif, reminiscent of how his ancestor Acrisius was killed).

To make a long story a bit shorter: Sthenelus, brother of Elektryon, now seized the territory of Mycenae, banished Amphitryon to Thebes in Boeotia, and gave the nearby district of Midea to Atreus and Thyestes, the sons of Pelops. The complicated saga of intra-familiar maneuverings that frames the Heracles story was of compelling interest to people in the areas involved, it is clear. It also fits a larger pattern of conflict between the eastern and western parts of the Peloponnese, probably relevant in the second-millennium BC Mycenaean period, when Pylos (in the far west) and Mycenae were both major power centers. We can glimpse, then, in the Heracles saga at this point, two key contrasts with the more folktale-inflected quest stories – its historical relevance, and also its compulsive tying together of family genealogies, a characteristic of Greek hero myths in general.

The adolescence of Heracles has portents of greatness but also signs of dangerous lack of control. For having struck him, he killed his music teacher Linus, a brother of Orpheus, with his own lyre. When he was eighteen, he killed a lion that had been attacking his father's cattle. This episode brought him into contact with a local aristocrat Thespius and every one of his fifty daughters (brought to bed with the young hero to take advantage of his divine stock). Heracles cuts the ears, noses, and hands off men of another Boeotian city who were tasked with getting a legal tribute from Thebes and defeats their fellow citizens in the ensuing war. But his marriage to Megara, as reward from the Thebans, led to disaster: driven mad by the ever-jealous Hera he threw his children into the hearth fire. After purification for the crime and self-imposed exile, Heracles settled in Tiryns, where his cousin Eurystheus, now ruling (thanks to Hera's intervention at their respective births), imposed on him the Labors.

It is not necessary here to catalogue these famous tasks, from the Nemean Lion to the Apples of the Hesperides. They inspired hundreds of artistic representations in ancient art. So, too, did the more erotic episodes in Heracles' subsequent career, such as his love for the young man Hylas, whom he accompanied on Jason's Argonaut expedition, not to mention his enforced servitude to Omphale, queen of the Lydians. Sold abroad for having unjustly murdered yet again, Heracles fought wars on Omphale's behalf – or, more notoriously, did women's work in her house while dressed in female garb. The transvestism has been interpreted in terms of initiation rituals (where young men cross-dress as a mark of transition), or as a political critique of decadent Eastern-style luxury. More boldly, the experiences of Heracles himself have been compared to the stories associated with archaic hunting-priests of the type know as "shamans." This social role, still practiced among some people of Central Asia and the Arctic, involves a trance-like Otherworld journey by the priest to supplicate divine masters of animals dwelling under the sea or at the ends of the world, so that they will provide food. Walter Burkert has seen in the boundary-beating excursions of Heracles to the extremes of the earth – whether the Pillars of Heracles at Gibraltar, or the underworld to fetch Cerberus, dog of Hades – a parallel to shamanic voyages. That Heracles dresses in animal skin, captures animals from monsters and brings them back alive (e.g. the Cattle of Geryon), and goes into sudden bouts of "madness" (trances?) makes Burkert think the Greek hero could preserve distant memories of shamanic practices.

The death of Heracles combines traces of his relation to the wild with a pathos-filled love-story and finally, an uplifting moral message – or at least one that was taken that way already in the fifth century BC. In a paradoxical and unwitting way, he might be said to have killed himself. Traveling with his second wife, Deianeira, in western Greece, he yielded to Nessus, a Centaur (a half-horse, half-man creature, not usually friendly to mortals) who insisted on carrying the woman across the river Euenus, as it was his right to ferry all comers. Halfway across, Nessus tried to rape Deianeria but was shot by Heracles, using an arrow poisoned with the Hydra's blood. The dying Nessus instructed the woman to make a potion from his blood and spilt semen, which would win the love of her husband whenever she thought it might be on the wane. Some years later, when Heracles was returning from his conquest of Oichalia with a war-prize, the young woman Iole, his apprehensive wife resorted to smearing the potion on a robe. When he donned it at a victory sacrifice, the poison seared his flesh leaving Heracles in agony. At an oracle's command, he was taken to the top of Mt. Oita and placed with his armor on a pyre, which was then ignited by sudden lightning. No bones were found. He had become an immortal, said the oracle.

Although the Athenians claimed to be the first to institute sacrifices to Heracles, his cult was indisputably Panhellenic. At the same time as he was accorded heroic honors, however, stories were told about the apotheosis ("turning into a god") of Heracles, with further strange details, such as his post-mortem reconciliation with Hera. Zeus persuaded his wife to adopt his illegitimate son, which she did by passing the hero through her legs in imitation of giving birth. As goddess of marriage, she then joined him to Eternal Youth (*Hêbê*). Thus Heracles came to embody fully the concept of antagonism between a god and mortal. He grew to deserve the seemingly ironic name of "the glory of Hera" by constantly struggling against the goddess in life, but becoming allied to her after death. You don't sharpen a knife on wood: in effect, it was Hera's stone-like resistance that both whetted Heracles and, when he surpassed all expectations, won renown for herself. The career of Heracles, in this guise of an ultimate success story, turned the hero into a moral exemplar. Prodicus, a sophist of the late fifth century BC, wrote an allegorical *The Choice of Heracles* featuring two women, Vice and Virtue, who offer the hero pathways to happiness (the former easy, the latter – which he took – arduous). Cicero refers to Hercules (the Latin form of the name) as a model for self-sacrifice that benefits the greater good. In the Middle Ages and Renaissance, the allegory became extremely popular, appearing in a twelfth-century poem by Peter of Blois and depicted in numerous emblem-books and paintings. So it is that in the thousands of years which saw the development of this particular hero-myth, its protagonist morphed from Paleolithic hunter to philosophical ideal.

Figure 3.3 The rough and ready Heracles had already been turned into an
          example of moral rectitude by the fifth century BC. Annibale Carracci
          (1596) depicts the hero's allegorical "choice" whether to follow
          Virtue and ascend her arduous path, or Vice, who points him toward
          ease and pleasures

Source: ART333918 Carracci, Annibale (1560–1609). Hercules at the Crossroads. Photo:
Luciano Pedicini, 1999. Location: Museo Nazionale di Capodimonte, Naples, Italy. Photo
Credit: Alinari/Art Resource, NY.

HERO AS POLITICIAN

> The deeds of Theseus are a spurre to prowess, and a glass
> How princes' sons and noblemen their youthful days should passe.
> > (Arthur Golding, dedicatory epistle to his
> > translation of Ovid, *Metamorphoses*, 1565)

Studying hero stories for their uplifting educational values – a
trend afoot already in Classical Athens, as we have just seen – also
tended to weed out details that might be unseemly for a teen-
age audience. At the same time, a demand for graphic action and
excitement nevertheless ensured that grittier details survived, creating a dynamic tension between acceptable and edgier treatments

of the hero, even in antiquity. We, too, still have a "choice of Heracles" – whether to watch the 1997 Disney cartoon version *Hercules*, which omits the madness, averted rape, and cremation, or the bloodier Brett Ratner-directed *Hercules* of 2014 (starring Dwayne "the Rock" Johnson).

Another feature that has been erased or ignored in later treatments of hero myths is their role in the politics of individual city-states. This aspect was not so much a threat to young minds as simply misunderstood once the relevant conditions had passed. Just as the Heracles saga sought to make a case for a certain view of regional politics in the Peloponnese and beyond, so the legends about Theseus shifted with various changes in regime at Athens to make Theseus stand for the values of the moment.

The offspring of the Athenian king Aegeus and Aethra, a woman from Troizen, 100 miles to the southwest on the Saronic Gulf, Theseus grew up in his mother's care and upon reaching manhood, went to find his father. After a series of adventures, he arrived to discover Aegeus now married to the ubiquitous Medea, who attempted to poison him (wishing her new son Medus to inherit). The tokens of identity – sandal and sword – that Aegeus had left under a rock in Troizen, and Theseus now bore, saved him. Now the crown prince of Athens, Theseus volunteered to end the human tribute (fourteen youths) sent every nine years to Minos of Crete. Having defeated there the half-man, half-bull Minotaur, and fled with the king's daughter Ariadne, whose clever thread device helped him out of the labyrinth, Theseus returned to Athens. But he inadvertently prompted his father's suicide when he failed to change the black sail on his ship to white, as he had promised, to signal victory. (He also forgot or abandoned Ariadne along the way, but the god Dionysos found her on Naxos and took up with her.)

None of this seems particularly politicized, although it may contain a vague memory of Athenian-Cretan relations in the Mycenaean period. Perhaps, like the Trojan War saga, the kernel of the Theseus myth began in the second millennium. What looks more pointed, however, are the details that accumulated around this core. Theseus is said to have brought the scattered communities within Attica (the 1,000-square-mile area around Athens) under one central government. He established the Isthmian Games, adding contests dedicated to Poseidon (widely rumored to be his real father) to an established ritual event near Corinth. Myth ignores chronology here, as the games were traditionally said to be established in the early sixth century BC, some six centuries after the supposed lifetime of Theseus.

The Athenian hero also was credited with winning a series of contests himself during his youthful journey from Troizen to Athens. His labors were performed explicitly in emulation of the older hero, Heracles (a distant cousin), according to Plutarch's second-century AD *Life of Theseus*. Individual details give them much more weight, however, than generic animal-baiting or villain-dispatching. At Epidaurus he slew Periphetes, a club-wielding highwayman. At the Isthmus of Corinth, he killed Sinis the Pine Bender by applying the ruffian's own method of yoking a victim between two flexible trees and releasing them. Sciron, a robber at Megara, he hurled off a cliff. Here we have a hint of the non-Athenian side of the story: as Plutarch reports, writers from Megara claimed Sciron was actually a good man, who punished robbers, and a relative of the famously righteous family of Achilles. On closer inspection, it emerges, every spot at which Theseus is said to have overcome local villains turns out to be a place to which Athens, in historical times, lay claim. And many of the "villains" encountered by Theseus turn out to have been heroes venerated by their own communities. Theseus, in other words, embodied Athenian imperial ambitions.

Theseus got credited with creating various Athenian institutions, such as the festival of the Oschophoria. Backed up by the tale that Theseus on embarking for Crete had disguised two young men as women (to increase his martial force), this annual ritual procession was led by two similarly attired young men (initiatory transvestism, again) but honored Dionysos and Ariadne – an odd detail given the hero's treatment of his erstwhile beloved, and an indication that an old festival of the vintage season had been rejiggered to celebrate Theseus. He also established a shrine of Aphrodite Pandemos ("of all the people") near the Acropolis – a name with hints of propaganda. The consummate politician, Theseus was said, as well, to have invented the ritual formula that opened each session of the Athenian assembly; to have given up absolute rule in favor of something more democratic; to have coined money; and to have aided Heracles, his idol, in a campaign against the Amazons, fierce warrior women from the East, capturing their princess. The lattermost boomeranged when the Amazons laid siege to Athens for three months, engaging in pitched battles right at the Acropolis.

Historians and archaeologists can peer through this fabric of fabulation to glimpse some actual events and political figures. The battle with the Amazons, for one, was clearly played up in the fifth century right after the Greek victory over the massed forces of the East led by the Persians. In myth, it was said that Theseus was ultimately exiled (or removed himself) from Athens to Scyros, where he was killed by that island's king. In 476 BC, after the Persian Wars, the general Cimon (c. 510–450 BC) retrieved the bones of Theseus and brought them back to Athens. The shrine which he built to house them was decorated with paintings that associated Theseus' mythical adventures (against Amazons, Centaurs, and Cretans) with the recent Athenian struggles. Theseus was thus made once more into the embodiment of the city-state and its success. A generation later, marble panels sculpted to decorate the west side of the great Parthenon of Athena depicted the Amazonomachy, while those on the temple's south wall showed Theseus battling the half-horse Centaurs.

The hero of Athens in its brief democratic heyday during the fifth century BC had also flourished under previous regimes. Solon, who made attempts to democratize Athens in the early sixth century BC, was credited with a *synoikismos* (uniting scattered villages of Attica), and with redesigning the city's major festival, the Panathenaia – just as Theseus had – which is to say, Solon's deeds were mythologized backwards onto the great hero of the past. Some years after Solon, Peisistratus, a "tyrant" (the word merely denotes a non-hereditary one-man ruler) who came to power in 546 BC, invoked Theseus' Cretan quest when he reorganized a festival of Apollo on the island of Delos – one of the hero's supposed stopping-points on the way back to his homeland.

HEROINE AS ATHLETE

Just because women were restricted from participating in political life, narrowly conceived (as in most democracies even until the twentieth century), does not mean that they had no effect in Greek *polis* life. Especially in cults that were largely celebrated by women – those of Demeter and Persephone, and some rites of Dionysos – the key importance of female religious activity for the well-being of the state was recognized. On the level of heroine myths, important roles were also imagined. We know that the idea of woman as athlete was not in itself a pure fantasy, as girls in Sparta and in the initiation cults of Artemis in Athens raced and competed in sports – albeit not at big public festivals like the Olympic Games. To help keep in mind the unexpected and creative power of heroic myths, it is worthwhile to conclude with the story of Atalantê.

Her name ("Equal on the scale") already says a lot. In the language of Homeric epic, this adjective is regularly applied to male heroes (Aeneas, Odysseus) who are "equal" to Zeus or Ares in strength or skill. Atalantê can be taken that way, but also, as the "equal" of any man. In a version of her myth current in rural Arcadia, she was abandoned and exposed as a child (like heroes in Raglan's template) and suckled by a she-bear. (Some say she reconnected with her birth-parents later.) A proud virgin and huntress, she came to resemble her protectress, Artemis, the goddess of wild animals. When two Centaurs tried to rape her, she shot them dead. At funeral games held for the father of Jason, she beat Peleus (father-to-be of Achilles) in wrestling. She participated, too, in that gathering of famous heroes, the boar hunt at Calydon, where she was first to wound the beast with her arrows.

Atalantê's superiority enabled her to set the rules of a foot-race to determine who might marry her. Giving her suitors a half-course head start, she then pursued them in full armor, striking down any she overtook. Only Melanion (or Hippomenes – names vary) manages to distract her by coming to the racecourse armed with three golden apples acquired from Aphrodite the love-goddess. When Atalantê stoops to pick up the strategically dropped fruit, Melanion wins the race, and her as his bride. Their end is appropriately emblematic both of the remarkably transgressive nature of the whole story (a woman beating men!) and of the heroine's affiliation with the natural world of the virgin Artemis. When out hunting, Atalantê and her new husband stop to make love in a sacred precinct, either of Zeus or of the Great Mother, Cybele, and for their impiety are turned into lions.

An interesting twist can serve as coda and also reminder that mythology thoroughly permeated everyday life for Greek men and women – which is how it grew and survived. One ecological niche for tale-telling and mythic allusion was the traditional Greek drinking party known as the *symposion* ("drinking together" – source of our *symposium*). And one accompaniment to such parties of upper-class Greek males was flirtation with adolescent boys: the custom of homo-erotic activity between older and younger males that we see depicted in the dialogues of Plato and on many Athenian vase-paintings was accepted among the elite as an educational institution that intro-duced boys to the world of men. (Meanwhile, the older men would normally have wives and perhaps courtesans, as well.) Sex and favors, courting-gifts (hares, fighting-cocks) and poetry were part of the system of male erotic behavior. It happens that we have some poems stemming from this sort of interaction in a book attributed to the sixth-century BC poet Theognis. One set of such verses, addressed to an older man's young would-be lover, turns Atalantê into a mythic exemplar, as it makes a prediction about the next stage in their relationship:

> Boy, don't wrong me. I still want to please you, and I make this observa-tion with all good cheer. Rest assured, you will not get the better of me nor will you trick me. For though you have won and have the advantage hereafter, yet I shall wound you as you flee from me, as they say once the daughter of Iasius, the maiden Iasie, who was ripe for marriage, refused men and fled. Girding herself, blonde Atalanta left her father's home and tried to accomplish what was not to be accomplished. She went off to the lofty mountain peaks, fleeing from lovely marriage, the gift of golden Aphrodite. But in the end she came to know it, in spite of her refusal.

> (Theognis 1287–94, trans. D. Gerber)

FURTHER READING

Good starting points on the topic of heroes are Walter Burkert, *Greek Religion*, trans. John Raffan (Cambridge, MA: Harvard University Press, 1985); Emily Kearns, *The Heroes of Attica* (London: University of London, Institute of Classical Studies, 1989); and Gunnel Ekroth, "Heroes and Hero-Cults," in D. Ogden (ed.),

A Companion to Greek Religion (Malden: Wiley-Blackwell, 2007): 100–114. A fascinating subcategory has been explored by Corinne Pache, *Baby and Child Heroes in Ancient Greece* (Urbana: University of Illinois Press, 2004). On the continuing efforts to heroize humans, see *New Heroes in Antiquity: From Achilles to Antinoos* by Christopher Jones (Cambridge, MA: Harvard University Press, 2010). For comparative studies on ancestor cults, see Timothy Insoll, "Ancestor cults," in T. Insoll, (ed.) *Oxford Handbook of the Archaeology of Ritual and Religion* (Oxford: Oxford University Press, 2011): 1043–1058.

Heroines are lucky to have two excellent studies devoted to them: Jennifer Larson, *Greek Heroine Cults* (Madison: University of Wisconsin Press, 1995), and Deborah Lyons, *Gender and Immortality: Heroines in Ancient Greek Myth and Cult* (Princeton: Princeton University Press, 1997). For the paradoxical status of one heroine, see the essays in James Clauss and Sarah Johnston (eds.), *Medea: Essays on Medea in Myth, Literature, Philosophy, and Art* (Princeton: Princeton University Press, 1997).

The dual vision concerning heroes in Homer and Hesiod is brilliantly articulated by Gregory Nagy in *The Best of the Achaeans* (Baltimore: Johns Hopkins University Press, 2nd. edn, 1999). On the archaeological record, see the rigorous analysis by Carla Antonaccio, *An Archaeology of Ancestors, Tomb Cult and Hero Cult in Early Greece* (Lanham: Rowman & Littlefield, 1995). On Odysseus cult in Ithaca, a good summary is given by Helen Waterhouse, "From Ithaca to the *Odyssey*," *The Annual of the British School at Athens* (91) 1996: 301–317.

On the literary reception of Sophocles' *Antigone*, there is an erudite survey by George Steiner, *Antigones* (New Haven: Yale University Press, 1996). On the dynamics of the ancient drama, see Charles Segal's essay on *Antigone* in Erich Segal (ed.) *Greek Tragedy: Modern Essays in Criticism* (New York: Harper & Row, 1983). Lowell Edmunds provides a comparative folkore study of another figure made famous by Sophocles in *Oedipus: The Ancient Legend and Its Later Analogues* (Baltimore: Johns Hopkins University Press, 1985). For the dramas about Iphigenia, see Donald J. Mastronarde, *The Art of Euripides: Dramatic Technique and Social Context* (Cambridge: Cambridge University Press, 2010).

Jason's role in the Hellenistic epic is meticulously analyzed by James Clauss, *The Best of the Argonauts: The Redefinition of the Epic*

Hero in Book 1 of Apollonius's Argonautica, (Berkeley: University of California Press, 1993). On Perseus, a fine survey is Daniel Ogden, *Perseus* (New York: Routledge, 2008). In the same very helpful series (*Gods and Heroes of the Ancient World*) one can find the broad-ranging *Herakles* by Emma Stafford (New York: Routledge, 2012). On Heracles and shamanism, see Walter Burkert's Sather Classical Lectures, *Structure and History in Greek Mythology and Ritual* (Berkeley: University of California Press, 1979). The political significance of Theseus is explored in essays collected by Anne Ward (ed.), *The Quest for Theseus* (New York: Praeger, 1970).

Finally, some context for Atalantê and gendered athletics is provided by Betty Spears, "A Perspective of the History of Women's Sport in Ancient Greece," *Journal of Sport History*, 11 (1984). The verses from Theognis concerning Atalantê are translated in Douglas E. Gerber, *Greek Elegiac Poetry from the Seventh to the Fifth Centuries* BC (Loeb Classical Library 258, Cambridge, MA: Harvard University Press, 1999).

4

INTERPRETING MYTHS

SYMBOLS AND SOCIETIES

Sex, violence, and pagan gods. Looking at myths from Greece and Rome, a Christian of the second or third century AD might have summed up the older tradition in this way. As we saw at the end of Chapter 1, he or she would not have been alone in such evaluation. Even earlier in antiquity interpreters of myth were already trying to excuse or explain away the first two characteristics. (The third, a multiplicity of gods, was of course not "pagan" to them.) When not simply denigrated as unworthy to be uttered, or as insulting to an elevated view of the divine, myths were allegorized or rationalized. Both methods proved their sturdiness as tools to circumscribe the power of these tales, although Christian authorities preferred the latter. We'll examine several key instances here. While inoculating readers – especially the young – against the danger of myths, they also preserved the myths for later generations by incorporating ancient myths into new forms of poetry and prose with a Christian slant.

The Renaissance and early modern periods saw a shift in approach, however. Rather than getting rid of myths or turning them into an innocuous kind of enigmatic language, readers of the old narratives in the fourteenth through the seventeenth centuries could begin to integrate their experience of the myths within a larger picture of the history and customs of the ancient Greeks and Romans. Myths were part of *culture*, to be taken as seriously as law, economics, and religion (from the last of which they were often inseparable.) A constant stream of new discoveries – of manuscripts, artworks, ancient material objects and archaeological monuments – enabled people to construct a much more nuanced and appreciative understanding of the ancient stories.

With the eighteenth century, yet other windows were opened onto the world of ancient myth. Increasingly far-flung exploration and colonization brought Europeans into contact with "primitive" peoples whose indigenous stories sounded remarkably similar to the myths that the incoming British or French, Dutch or Spanish had been taught in school. What could explain that? The newly organized sciences of anthropology and comparative linguistics began to offer answers. By the early nineteenth century, Romantic writers were celebrating and co-opting myths from all over the globe, partly in a reaction against Enlightenment disdain for non-rational thought, partly in search of an alternative to more repressive forms of Christianity, and mainly out of pure enjoyment of the sensuous and exotic. Contemporary approaches to mythology today owe something to all of these stages – more than some practitioners may want to acknowledge. In what follows we shall concentrate the analysis on several of the most productive modern ways of thinking about Classical myths. In so doing, two forms of continuity overarching the centuries need to be stressed: the view of myths as symbolic; and the notion that they have something to say about society.

MYTHS AS SYMBOLS: GREEKS TO ROMANTICS

For Christian writers of the second century AD, the pagan myths were the most obvious target in any attempt to argue for the superiority of their own new religion. Several strategies had to be developed to counter, or at least defuse, the glamorous appeal of gods and heroes. These tales in the poeticized versions by Homer, Vergil, and the dramatists had for centuries been the centerpiece of education of the Greek and Roman elite, the very social classes that expanding Christianity needed to reach.

One strategy was to use the scandalous pre-existing stories to prove that the unconverted pagans *already* had invested in some basic feature of Christian dogma. They just had to rid themselves of the impure trappings of such tales (insulting as these were to true divinity) in order to fully believe the new narrative. One important Christian apologist (someone who defends and explains the faith) was Justin, a highly educated Greek speaker from what is now Nablus in Palestine. In his *First Apology* (c. AD 155–57), addressed to the Roman emperor Antoninus Pius (ruled AD 138–61), Justin asserted that a belief in Christ's ascension into heaven was nothing new, compared to what pagans already accepted. Dionysos, Perseus, Asclepius, Heracles, Castor, and Pollux – one could draw up a long list of pagan gods and heroes who had similar post-mortem experiences. Ariadne and others after all had even been transformed by the gods into constellations of stars ("katasterism" was the technical term). "And what about those emperors of yours who die, whom you judge worthy of being deified, trotting out someone who swears he saw Caesar rise to heaven from his funeral after being cremated?" (Ch. 21)

Yet Justin was apparently conscious that scholarly pagan opponents could flip such an argument on its head, arguing for their part that Christ was just another fable like their story of Hercules (to use his Latin name more familiar in the West). To forestall such objections, he used a clever tale – mythic in its own motifs – about wicked trickster "demons." (Justin employs the ancient Greek term for "minor divinities" but gives it a Christian semantic twist to mean "bad *daimones*" – the origin of our English word.) These unnamed evil spirits, hearing from the ancient prophets about Christ's imminent arrival, had long ago plotted to deceive the human race by inventing such death-and-resurrection stories as Justin has listed, to convince people "that the things concerning Christ were just marvelous tales like those uttered by the poets" (Ch. 54). This rhetorical pincer movement meant to put sophisticated pagans on the spot may have convinced some, but unfortunately did not save Justin Martyr himself, who was executed around AD 165 with other Christians for refusing to make sacrifices to the gods of Rome.

Paradoxically, early Christian apologists had to *resist* the ancient Greek interpretive method of allegorizing away the gods. As we saw in Chapter 1, such thinkers as Prodicus were already in the fifth century BC explaining that "Demeter" and "Dionysos" were names for bread and wine. Pagan allegorizing enabled the Christians' opponents

Figure 4.1 On a Red-figure *lekythos* (460 BC), Ariadne sleeps beside Theseus, after the overcoming of the Minotaur in the Cretan labyrinth. A tiny Eros, sign of sexual attraction, rests at her head. Left on the island of Naxos by the Athenian hero, she later weds the god Dionysos and is commemorated through the constellation Corona Borealis, said to be the crown given by her divine husband

Source: AA389189 Ariadne and Theseus, from Athena waking Ariadne and Theseus, Red-figure lekythos (oil flask), c. 460 BC Classical Greek (detail) Location: Museo Nazionale Taranto, Photo Credit: Gianni Dagli Orti/The Art Archive at Art Resource, NY.

to slide out of their grasp whenever a direct assault was attempted on the immorality of ancient myths. "They're just symbols" must have been a frustrating but common response, it seems. On the other hand, if the Christians themselves resorted to allegorizing their opponents' gods, the tables would no doubt soon be turned on the story of Christ. The Christian apologist Tatian (c. AD 120–180), a pupil of Justin Martyr, therefore challenged the proponents of traditional paganism to defend their gods *without* allegorizing them: "If you do attempt this, their divinity amongst you is destroyed" says Tatian – the gods become a deceptive sort of fiction. From the apologist's rhetoric, it is clear that modern-sounding interpretation of myth as plain entertainment was already being practiced. Hector and Achilles, Helen and Paris "you will of course say are introduced just for the sake of literary structure (*oikonomia*), since not one of them existed." Tatian concludes by refusing to play their game, "for it is not right to compare our idea of God with people wallowing in matter and mud" (*Address to the Greeks*, Ch. 21).

The ongoing duel between Christians and pagans over the proper use of allegory seems to have driven both sides to keep refining and elaborating their interpretive methods, with important consequences for how myth was treated in subsequent centuries. Until the closing of the Academy of Plato by the Christian emperor Justinian in AD 529, the explication of the philosopher's subtle other-worldly ideas was carried on by a series of devoted scholars. Porphyry, a key philosopher and vocal opponent of the Christians (c. AD 234–305) used allegory to interpret Homer, as well, in Neo-Platonist terms. His remarkable short treatise survives on the cave of the Naiad nymphs mentioned in the *Odyssey* (*Od*.13.102–12). For Porphyry the cave itself represents the material world, its waters are the flux of matter and its darkness stands for the world's material obscurity. An olive tree planted nearby symbolizes the wisdom of Athena; even its leaves, tending upwards or downwards with the season, allude to the revolutions of souls in the world. When Odysseus deposits his possessions in the cave, we are being taught, in enigmatic symbols, that the soul must leave behind destructive passions. In short, the myth of Odysseus is the story of the soul's journey through life.

Such philosophical point-for-point allegorizing, when not directed at the nature of gods, seems to have been acceptable to Christians. The stories about Heracles, with their kaleidoscope of varied episodes, proved fertile ground for moralizing allegory no matter what the writer's religion. As we saw in Chapter 3, the interpretation of Heracles as a symbolic figure began very early. Apart from the already mentioned "choice of Heracles," the moralizing tale attributed to Prodicus, another writer of the fifth century BC, Herodorus of Pontus, interpreted the apples of the Hesperides as the three virtues of avoiding anger, love of money, and love of pleasure. Heracles' club was philosophy itself. A slightly later tradition made the Twelve Labors equivalent to signs of the zodiac, which Heracles – a symbol of the Sun itself – marched through in his victory. In words closer to Christian writing, the Stoic philosopher Epictetus (c. AD 55–135) asserted that nothing was more dear to the hero than his god. "For this reason it was believed that he was the son of Zeus, and he was. Obeying him he went all around purging away injustice and lawlessness" (*Discourses* 2.16.44). To Julian (the "Apostate" – AD 331–63), the emperor raised as a Christian who tried briefly to restore pagan Roman worship as the state religion, Heracles was a moral model. As a student of Neo-Platonism, he believed that "myths about the sacred cry out for us to analyze and track down hidden meanings" (*To the Cynic Heraclius*, 222d). He imagined himself as undergoing trials like those of his heroic exemplar, and several times cited the famous "choice" tale. So did a former classmate of his from their university days in Athens, Basil of Caesarea (AD 330–379), who went on to become a bishop (and eventually saint), referring to the same story in his essay recommending the virtues of pagan literature even for young Christian men.

Thanks to the cleansing powers of allegory, Hercules made it through the Middle Ages as the equivalent of a respected hero from the Bible, a Samson or a David who had faced monstrous Greek avatars of Goliath. Contributing mightily to his survival as a paradigmatic hero was the Latin poetry of Ovid (43 BC–c. AD 17). The *Metamorphoses* (to which we shall return in the next chapter) was the masterpiece of this brilliant Roman poet and the single most influential mythological collection in Western literature. This sometimes scandalous pagan poetry was made acceptable to a medieval Christian audience through a long series of allegorical treatments, starting in the twelfth century but based on sources from Late Antiquity (e.g. the mythographic writing of Fulgentius, early sixth century AD). Arnulf of Orléans (c. 1170) wrote a much-read commentary on the poem combining philological and allegorical approaches. An English émigré in Paris, John of Garland, around 1234 composed a poem in 520 elegiac verses, the *Coverings of Ovid* (*Integumenta Ovidii*) that promised to unveil the secret allegories of the poem. Early in the next century, *Moralized Ovid (Ovide Moralisé)* was produced by an anonymous writer, apparently at the request of the French royal court. Also in the fourteenth century, Ovid was the greatest single influence on the work of Geoffrey Chaucer (c. 1343–1400). For Coluccio Salutati (1331–1406), a humanist working in Florence in the same time period, the allegorized Hercules became a perfect Renaissance knight, a model to reform the education of young noblemen. In Renaissance France, Pierre de Ronsard composed a *Hymn to Christian Hercules* (1555) with eighteen parallels – sometimes far-fetched – between the ancient hero and Christ. Just as the Roman god Jupiter suspended time when he spent the night with Hercules' mother Alcmene, so it took three years to prepare the birth of Christ (lines 151–58); just as Hercules after death married Hebe, goddess of everlasting youth, Christ married Eternity; Hercules freed Prometheus from his rock; so Christ freed humanity from the bonds of sin – and so forth. In short, the symbolic approach to this one set of myths had a long and varied run. And Heracles/Hercules does not stand alone: similar interpretive attempts have been applied to just about every major story.

The interpretation of myths as symbols received new impetus in the Romantic period, starting in the later eighteenth century. Along with emerging nationalism in Germany, Italy, and France, a retreat from industrialization in England, and the re-discovery of older folk traditions all over Europe, went a fresh appreciation for the ancient stories that seemed to provide a counter-balance to the Enlightenment's obsession with rationality. New forms of modern critical discourse – philosophy, theology, the history of religion, literary study, and the proto-forms of anthropology, sociology, and psychology – took shape in the struggle to define and evaluate the myths (as has been well demonstrated by the intellectual historian Andrew von Hendy).

By the 1760s, the tired forms of moralizing allegory that treated ancient narratives as "fables" had lost their appeal, thanks to the rise of scientific explanations. Instead, the barbarous and archaic elements of such narratives began to exert a new fascination, precisely because their mysterious qualities *resisted* scientific explanation. "Myth" (from the ancient Greek term *muthos*, as we saw in Chapter 1) came to displace "fable" bringing along the added signification of *religious* importance. This new appeal to the power of myth resembled late antique Neo-Platonism (which itself was rediscovered in the eighteenth century), in which the stories that so scandalized Plato were rehabilitated through the magic of allegorical hermeneutics. German thinkers like Christian Gottlob Heyne (1729–1812) and Johann Gottfried Herder (1744–1803) led the way in re-purposing myth as an organic, holistic way of understanding life. The latter, in particular, understood myth not as moral tales dressed up in pretty terms but as a relic of primitive attempts, born out of fear, to understand and control the cosmos. Myth was a powerful combination, therefore, of religion, history, and pure poetry. Herder could envision it as inspiring a German literary renaissance – which soon proved true in the work of Goethe and Hölderlin. In England, Thomas Carlyle (1795–1881) praised Heyne as going further than any Classicist in penetrating into the ancients, "their Spirit and character, their way of life and thought" (*The Life of Heyne*, 1828). Samuel Taylor Coleridge (1772–1834) came to know Heyne and his ideas during a year at Göttingen (1798–99), an encounter that stimulated the poet's life-long engagement with mythology. Also influential for Coleridge and other Romantics was the philologist Friedrich Creuzer, whose ambitious *Symbolik und Mythologie* (1819) attempted to derive Greek myths from the works of Eastern sages. The suggestion that all myths were somehow universal and interconnected would reappear in the next century in the new discipline of psychoanalysis. Once more, German scholarship provided the bridge.

MYTHS AS SYMBOLS: FREUD, JUNG, AND OTHERS

Sigmund Freud (1856–1939) and Carl Gustav Jung (1875–1961), the two men whose work initiated the study of myths from the standpoint of psychology, grew up immersed in the tradition of late-nineteenth century German devotion to classical antiquity. Freud's wife Martha was a niece of the famous Classicist Jacob Bernays (1824-1881), an expert on the school of Aristotle. Jung's father, a Swiss Lutheran minister (who bore the middle name "Achilles"), was also a trained philologist. Both Freud and Jung could quote passages in Greek and Latin from memory, and their conversation and writing showed an easy familiarity with the ancient world. It was therefore not accidental that in their studies on the workings of the human mind both men turned first to the world of myth for analogies and examples, although neither had originally set out to explore this domain.

Freud, the son of a Jewish wool merchant, spent most of his life in Vienna, where he began work as a neurologist and later practiced and wrote about the revolutionary treatment method he termed "psychoanalysis." The first of his works to deal with myth in an important way, *The Interpretation of Dreams* (*Die Traumdeutung*, 1899), presented his theory that dreams are a psychologically necessary mechanism of wish-fulfillment. It was in this connection that Freud made his first public statement of what he came to call the "Oedipus complex." (He had raised the idea in private letters to his friend Wilhelm Fliess starting in 1897.) As he later came to elaborate the notion, Freud pinpointed the ages of three to five as the time when young boys develop a desire to get rid of their father and "possess" their mother. (An analogous father-daughter relationship he later named the "Electra complex," after the young woman who kills her mother Clytemnestra in the myths of the house of Atreus.) The outright expression of this desire is short-lived and eventually repressed; the growth involved in dealing with the complex represents a key developmental step for the child's psyche. But, for Freud, the marks of this struggle remain in each person's unconscious.

Characteristically, Freud combined personal clinical experience with literary sophistication in citing as evidence for the underlying desire the (alleged) frequent occurrence of the motif of incest in patients' dreams, and the powerful effect which the ancient Greek tale of Oedipus has always had on audiences. Freud's reading of the Oedipus story – which he equated with one deservedly famous version of the tale, the drama by Sophocles (c. 424 BC) is profound – but also profoundly problematic. The drama, first of all, focuses not on the actual story of how Oedipus unknowingly killed his father and married his mother, but on the discovery of these painful events by Oedipus, now king of Thebes, years after they happened. If anything, the play is more like a psychoanalytic session, dredging up and purging the past, than it is an enactment of desire. Second, as was pointed out in Chapter 3, when compared with other ancient versions of the Oedipus tale, and worldwide folktale renditions of the same motifs (parricide and incest), the full story of Oedipus is not in fact one of infamy, degradation, and revulsion, but rather a paradoxical meditation on the integrative powers of transgression.

Oedipus, seen at his death (as in Sophocles' last play, *Oedipus at Colonus*, 406 BC), becomes a holy and heroic protector of the territory that entombs him. Freud thus has privileged only part of the full tale. In his later career, he wove his own personal mythic version around the darkest side of the Oedipus tale, presenting in *Totem and Taboo* (1913) a theory about the origin of culture: a putative first parricide gave rise to feelings of remorse and guilt, shared by the horde of the sons of the father, and these feelings in turn, Freud speculated, produced all human moral sense, art, ethics, and religion.

The similarity between myth and dream has been noticed quite often, and was not a discovery of the twentieth century. Australian aboriginal peoples have traditionally made the connection explicit by referring to the "Dreamtime" as the primeval foundational period for the sacred stories that give structure to their landscape and belief-system. The major gain which Freudian psychology offers for the study of myth lies in the detailed analogy drawn between myth and dream as *processes*. Freud was first to delineate three specific operations occurring in dreams: condensation (the melding of various elements into a single symbolic expression); displacement (the substitution of one symbolic element for a different referent); and representation (the change of feelings and ideas into visual images). The psychoanalytic critic can refer to the same processes to explain the sometimes disturbing and bizarre elements in such stories as the Greek succession myth, with its motifs of chaos, castration, and swallowing of children. It is worth underlining here the essential but often overlooked continuity between the psychoanalytic approach and earlier attempts – going back to the sixth century BC – to interpret features of myth in allegorical terms. At bottom, both the ancient and modern methods rely on the notion of the *symbol* as the basis for how myth operates.

Richard Caldwell, the most sophisticated contemporary proponent of this brand of myth interpretation, applies it to the origin myths within the *Theogony* of Hesiod that we looked at in Chapter 2. Attempting to explain these stories by excavating their layers of unconscious contents related to the human life-cycle, Caldwell sees in the creation of Eros (Desire) and Gaia (Earth) that stage in which the infant differentiates itself from the mother, realizing its own wants and needs. In the stories of early tyrant gods being overthrown by their sons (Ouranos by Kronos by Zeus), one can detect a fantasy of Oedipal success, which the final winner (Zeus) then denies to any would-be usurper (cf. his swallowing of Mêtis to avoid having a child who is stronger than himself). In addition, Caldwell reads the ways in which Ouranos and Kronos try to keep their positions of patriarchal power as primarily narcissistic.

"Narcissism" as a term used for a stage in psychological growth (or an adult personality disorder) was popularized by Freud through an essay of 1914; its use to mean "the condition of gaining emotional or erotic gratification from self-contemplation" (as defined by the *Oxford English Dictionary*) of course is based on a figure from an ancient myth narrated most fully in Ovid's *Metamorphoses* (Book 3). Narcissus, a handsome sixteen-year-old Greek, rejected attempts by the nymph Echo to make love. (Echo's erotic pursuit faltered because she had already been cursed by Juno only to repeat others' last few words.) The young man was punished by falling in love with his own reflection in a pool of water. Unable to grasp and hold this, he pined away, turning into a white-petaled flower that bears his name. Ironically, in the case-study of the original sufferer, full emotional gratification was *not* attainable, causing his death (in other ancient versions, by suicide). The notion that being alone with oneself could actually be sometimes pleasurable looks like the Romantic love of solitude imposed on an ancient myth. It is not surprising that the *OED* cites as the first use of the term in English a letter by the poet Coleridge (Jan. 15, 1822): "Of course, I am glad to be able to correct my fears as far as public Balls, Concerts, and Time-murder in Narcissism."

The anthropologist Bronislaw Malinowski (see below) was an important early dissenter from the psychoanalytic approach. In 1923 he wrote:

> The infection by psycho-analysis of the neighboring fields of science – notably that of anthropology, folklore and sociology – has been a very rapid and somewhat inflammatory process. The votaries of Freud, or some among them, have displayed in their missionary zeal an amount of dogmatism and of aggressiveness not calculated to allay the prejudice and suspicion which usually greet every new extension of their theories
>
> (Malinowski, from a letter to the editor of *Nature*)

Malinowski's major criticism of Freud – that he overlooked important cultural differences – still stands: while proclaiming the universal character of the Oedipus complex, Freud was unaware that in New Guinea, for instance, given radically different family structures, the father plays little or no role as an object of psychological aggression.

Similar objections have been made against the assertions of universality which underlie the work of C. G. Jung, the second major figure whose theories make use of symbolic interpretations of myth. The Swiss psychologist was a close friend and collaborator with Freud from 1907 until 1913, when their differences over the role of sexuality in neurosis drove them apart. After the break, Jung developed the influential notions of "archetypes" and the "collective unconscious." The former were believed by Jung to be archaic remnants in human consciousness which gave rise to specific, regularly recurring types of motifs and images in both myth and dream. Where Freud had seen in dream imagery an unsystematic, uniquely personal expression of an individual's psychic disturbances, Jung saw the representation of regular patterns that belonged to a shared, "collective" psychic structure. Some of the many instinctual "archetypal" images Jung identified, as culturally formed instances of the unconscious "archetypes," are those of the mother and father, the trickster, the wise old man, the hero, and the *animus* or *anima*. This last pair is a unique contribution by Jung; by these terms he refers to the unconscious images that women form of men (*animus*) and men of women (*anima*). In another formulation, Jung describes the *anima* as the "feminine side" of a man, and even attributed problems of violence and war to an underdevelopment of this psychic facet in the modern world. Jung's occasional forays into the psychology of groups had unintended results at times: his remarks in the 1930s on differences between Germanic and Jewish "psyches" were taken as pro-Nazi, though Jung denied any such leanings.

Whether or not Jungian theory explains the *origin* of any given myth does not alter the success which his theories have had in therapeutic use, through which patients are taught to handle relationships with archetypes, recognizing how their unconscious repressions or projections stand in the way of psychological wholeness. Jung's influence has been overwhelming in the work of a twentieth-century American popularizer Joseph Campbell

(1904–1987). In *The Hero with a Thousand Faces* (1949) and many subsequent books, Campbell rummaged through worldwide mythology to construct a "monomyth" of the hero, knowledge of which, he claims, can help each person discover his or her individuality. A spate of Campbell-inspired self-help books and workshops turned the individual's quest for "inner" heroes and heroines into a profitable segment of popular psychologizing, in the process encouraging interpretation of myths as allegories of interior life. At the same time, Campbell has played an unexpected side role that connects various American myth-makers. A friend of John Steinbeck in the 1930s (known for his gritty realist novels *The Grapes of Wrath*, *Of Mice And Men*, and *Cannery Row*), Campbell four decades later influenced George Lucas, the Hollywood filmmaker, who has said he modified a draft of the "Star Wars" trilogy after reading *The Hero with a Thousand Faces*.

A different psychoanalytic interpretation of hero-myths was articulated by Otto Rank in *The Myth of the Birth of the Hero* (1909). As with Jung and Freud, the motivation for theorizing was the perceived close similarities among myths from widely disparate cultures. These had to be explained, it was thought, as reflexes of universally shared psychic processes. Rank tallies all the parallels he can find among heroes of folktale and myth, anticipating the work some decades later of Lord Raglan (discussed in Chapter 3).

But as opposed to the folklorist's or anthropologist's approach, in which the shared elements may reflect social practices or historical events, the psychoanalyst finds deeper unconscious reasons within human development for what seem to be universals. The common motif of the high-born hero's removal from his natal family was taken by Rank to illustrate "the family romance" of neurotics, an idea that Freud developed around the same time as Rank was writing. Recognizing that some patients markedly failed to liberate themselves from parental authority even in their adult life, Freud noted that it was common for pre-pubescent children, especially if slighted or feeling a lack of affection, to imagine that their "real" parents were persons *other than* the mother and father with whom they happened to live. This child's fantasy – that his or her "real" father was a millionaire, king, or hero – Freud read as a desire to regress to the child's youngest conscious memories, when their biological parents seemed godlike and perfect. Myths, for Rank, retained and exposed this retrograde desire, treating hero tales as a type of wish-fulfillment. In other words, through them adults could air the fantasies of their childhood, making themselves into heroes or heroines (the abandoned children who eventually succeed). From a different point of view, the explanation composed by Rank, with Freud's blessing, is itself yet another multiform of the persistent myth of the Golden Age, which already in the Hesiodic version (c. 700 BC), as we saw, had been generalized to represent an entire culture's lost, best years.

MYTHS AND SOCIETY: EARLY FORERUNNERS

So, we return once more to Hesiod. His *Theogony* and *Works and Days*, standing at the very start of recorded Greek mythology, seem to contain the seeds of the two main trunks of myth interpretation that this chapter traces. On the one hand, the narratives of violent succession of gods clearly lend themselves to Freudian psychoanalytic efforts. But, on the other hand, the desires and deeds of fiercely individual divinities yield, in Hesiod's account, to the building of society – first, the harmonious Olympian order established (with some flexing of muscle) by Zeus; then, the society of humans – shaped and forever marked by Zeus' duel of wits with his cousin Prometheus.

The other major ancient method for dealing with inconvenient features of myth was Euhemerism, as we saw in Chapter 1 – the theory that gods were really just early humans who were elevated to divine status for their great accomplishments. At its core, this rationalizing approach was essentially historical. It was therefore unlike the free-floating, often subjective method of viewing myths in terms of allegories and symbols. After all, saying that there had existed such brilliant mortals led naturally to questions about where and when they lived. Just as the allegorical approach continued into modern times under a new guise (psychoanalysis), so, too, ancient rationalizing branched out into several forms of contemporary modes, in particular the sociological. While there are fewer examples of the social and historical interpretation of myths during the Middle Ages and Renaissance, it starts to make headway in the seventeenth and eighteenth centuries, becoming as dominant as the symbolic mode in the nineteenth, and the favored scholarly method in the twenty-first, although pop psychology still retains some ground for the symbol-hunting method.

The early modern versions are connected in spirit with another strain in ancient Greek thinking, which deserves some mention first. In his Five Ages, Hesiod takes his audience from the paradise-like conditions of the lost Golden Age to the gritty Iron Age conditions of the poet's present day. This fits the didactic stance of the archaic poet, who argues for a sense of justice despite the corrupt practices that he sees all around. There was a competing vision, however, even in antiquity. As early as the sixth century, Xenophanes, known for his critique of mythology (as seen in Chapter 1), wrote "The gods did not reveal, from the beginning, everything to mortals, but they [i.e. mortals], in the course of time, by searching add to the discovery of what is better" (fr. 18). In other words, the philosopher believes in human progress, rather than mythical decline. Xenophanes does not give particular examples (although from other surviving quotes it seems he spoke of coinage, a fairly recent invention of the Lydians, and astronomical research). A more detailed list of the inventions that mark human progress is the striking speech put in the mouth of the main character in the fifth-century BC drama attributed to Aeschylus (c. 525–456 BC), *Prometheus Bound* (lines 442–71). Unable to free himself from the suffering he endures at the hands of Zeus as punishment for stealing fire, the god recalls all the benefactions he had given mortals. Before his intervention they were helpless like infants; not knowing how to build, they lived underground like ants (perhaps an Aeschylean hint at autochthony myths). But Prometheus taught them to anticipate the seasons by watching the movement of stars, along with numbers, writing, animal husbandry, and sailing. Although this version does not specify that humans themselves came up with such helpful inventions, it is certainly a tale of increasing civilization and comfort.

A third ancient testimony to the notion of progress comes from another fifth-century thinker, Democritus of Abdera in northern Greece (c. 460–370 BC). Best known today for his idea that the material world is made of indivisible atoms, he also wrote on a range of subjects including, it appears, the origins of culture (what we would call anthropology). As extrapolated from some meager surviving sources, Democritus held that humans in prehistoric times lived a primitive existence, surviving on fruits and herbs. Forced to band together to ward off animal attacks, they developed spoken languages (different ones for each small group). The arts of preserving food and taming fire made possible their leap to civilization – a combination of motifs that sounds like a distant echo of the intertwined myths of the fire-bringing Prometheus and Pandora with her storage jar.

The historical reality of myths was taken for granted by many writers in ancient times, as it must have been for the citizens of Greek city-states and of Rome. After all, no matter how one might wish to allegorize the doings of gods, especially when they appeared to be immoral, it was a riskier, even unpatriotic act to deny that the place you lived was actually founded by a noble ancient hero, whether Aeneas (ancestor of the Romans) or Odysseus (founder of many settlements in southern Italy). The Trojan War, also, was for the Athenian historian of the late fifth century BC, Thucydides (in other regards an astute critic of mythology), unquestionably a matter of real history. Ironically, the story of the war drifted into the realm of fable and unfounded myth in later ages, only to be rediscovered as an historical plausibility toward the end of the nineteenth century, when the wealthy merchant and self-taught archaeologist Heinrich Schliemann (1822–1890) uncovered traces of a great city on the east coast of the Aegean Sea, close to where tradition had located Troy. No single piece of evidence has irrefutably identified the spot as the famed Homeric city, but spectacular finds of gold jewelry, bronze weapons, and impressive fortifications all seem to confirm the epic picture of a flourishing citadel and surrounding town that fell suddenly to a disaster – war, fire, or both.

A century and a half before Schliemann's spade initiated the archaeological positivism that would turn the old epic poets into transmitters of historical facts, two important thinkers, almost exact contemporaries, had raised the possibility that myth embodied real experiences from the past. Bernard Le Bovier de Fontenelle (1657–1757), a nephew of the dramatist Corneille, completed around 1690 an essay *On the Origin of Fables* (not published until 1724). He began from the idea that the earliest humans were too unsophisticated to have invented allegories. Therefore the myths that they told must represent an attempt to understand their immediate environment. Because their experience was so limited, however, the first myth-makers arrived at a mixture of poetic imaginings (for instance that the sun was a god, or stars were transformed human beings) and basic mistakes. Nevertheless, the record of the misunderstanding was *itself* a history of mentality, a window into a far-distant era. Fontenelle's conclusion – "Let us not seek anything else in fables but the history of the errors of the human mind" – is therefore not a dismissal but a real call for understanding an alien, "mythic" mode of thinking. In approaching myths this way he in fact anticipated French thinkers of the twentieth century, such as Lucien Lévy-Bruhl (1857–1939), author of *How Natives Think* (1910) and Claude Lévi-Strauss (1908–2009; see further below), whose many books (e.g. *The Savage Mind*, 1962) found, in the narratives of traditional people, a highly systematic manner of reasoning that happened to be mostly alien to Western ways of knowing. Fontenelle was also ahead of his time in recognizing that the newly discovered tribal peoples of Africa and North America possessed cultures that could fruitfully be juxtaposed with those of the ancient Classical world. His work therefore can be seen as foreshadowing later eighteenth-century discoveries in comparative linguistics as well as the typological study of law and social systems.

Giambattista Vico of Naples (1668–1744) differed from Fontenelle in maintaining a theory of history as cyclical, rather than linear. In his *New Science* (1725) Vico developed the notion that human history could be divided into the three ages: of gods, heroes, and men. Each period gave way to its successor age after a struggle for power (another Hesiodic touch). Each had its own political situation, distinctive language, laws, and customs. Vico freely uses tales from Homeric poetry to argue for earlier ways of life, seeing, for example, in the world of the Cyclops described in Book 9 of the *Odyssey* an early stage of civilization before partnerships or villages existed. Most important, each of Vico's hypothetical ages featured a different set of cognitive skills. The earliest humans "thought in poetic characters and spoke in fables" (Bk. 2, section 429). Metaphor therefore played a crucial role in the very development of language. Rather than being a sophisticated device used by later poets to disguise the real (physical or moral) meanings of myth in attractive garb, the myths themselves were products of a more primitive, childlike mentality in which sequences of visual imagery expressed more abstract ideas. The story of the killing by Cadmus of the monstrous Python in Thebes, for example, condensed into a few images a primitive observation about the development of agriculture: the dragon's teeth sown in the ground actually signify the hard woods necessary for breaking up soil before the invention of the iron plowshare; the armed men that sprang up from the sowing signify the uniting of people in stable communities for defense (sect. 335). Vico may sound like an allegorist interpreter of myth, but the essential difference is that in his view, the original employment of mythic metaphors was a mental necessity, not a literary choice. Just as important, it was universal, not the possession of an educated elite. For this reason, he equated *la sapienza poetica* ("poetic wisdom") with *la sapienza volgare* ("popular wisdom").

In retrospect, a number of nineteenth-century writers on myth followed in Vico's footsteps, consciously or not. Vico's own interest in the lore of "primitive" peasants of the Cilento region of Campania finds a parallel in the work of the early Romantic essayist and antiquarian Herder (see above), whose work in turn provided impetus for the collecting and rewriting of folktales by the brothers Jacob and Wilhelm Grimm. These men were united by the notion that "the folk" (rural, illiterate, and permanently settled in one place) represented a source of timeless wisdom. In effect, their interest was outward-looking and anthropological, as opposed to the inward, philosophical interests of those who interpreted myth by way of symbols and allegories.

MYTHS AND SOCIETY: THE ROLE OF RITUAL

The modern science of anthropology took root in Britain in the second half of the nineteenth century. At the peak of empire, the country was flooded with information about the customs and beliefs of newly encountered peoples in the distant lands visited by British merchants, soldiers, and missionaries. It may be that a similar expansion of exploration, travel, and colonization by Greeks from the eighth to fifth centuries BC, had encouraged their first attempts at describing other people's myths, in such fifth-century writers as Herodotus and Democritus. Just as the Greeks' encounter with new societies contributed to a growing cultural relativism in the Classical period, so in Britain the invention of modern anthropology coincided with some implicit criticism of established faith.

The career of William Robertson Smith (1846–1894), a founder of the discipline, well illustrates how this environment influenced the interpretation of myth. Brought up in a strict Scottish household,

son of a Free Church secessionist minister, Smith became a controversial scholar of Semitic languages, who was removed in 1881 from
his Chair of Hebrew and Old Testament Exegesis at the Free Church
College in Aberdeen because church authorities thought his teach-
ings might cause divinity students to lose their faith. (Heresy charges
brought against him were later dropped.) He became an editor of the
Encyclopaedia Britannica and later Professor of Arabic at Cambridge. In
a series of books starting in 1881, he suggested, among other things,
that Arabs and Hebrews originally lived in matrilineal societies. His
most influential work, *Lectures on the Religion of the Semites* (1889),
undertook to show that ritual practices such as animal sacrifice originated prior to religious dogmas: Hebrew sacrifice, he argued, rather
than being a sin-offering or covenant with a higher God, began as a
ritual for uniting clans with their tribal god through the eating of an
ordinarily forbidden "totem" animal.

Smith's theories scandalized many in his day, and are not accepted
by current historians of religion. But they did have a great effect
on a friend and fellow Scot, James George Frazer (1854–1941), the
first person ever to hold a university chair in social anthropology.
Frazer, son of a well-to-do Glasgow merchant family, studied
classical literature at Glasgow University and later as a fellow of
Trinity College, Cambridge. Throughout his scholarly life, he
worked on classical texts, producing editions of the Greek travel
writer Pausanias, the mythographer Apollodorus, and the *Fasti* of
the Roman poet Ovid. But his real interest lay in the obscure cults
and customs described by these ancient authors. In 1890, Frazer
published in two volumes *The Golden Bough: A Study in Comparative
Religion*. In it, he set out to answer two seemingly simple questions,
about a custom described by Strabo (5.3.12) and a fourth-century
AD commentator on Vergil's *Aeneid* (Servius on *Aen.* 6.136): why
was the priest at Nemi in Aricia obliged to kill his predecessor and
why, before doing so, had he to pluck a branch of the sacred grove
there (which Frazer speculated was the "Golden Bough" mentioned
in Vergil)?

Frazer's answer, elaborated over the next twenty-five years, was
that the priest represented an original sacred king, whose required
death and revival (in the form of a new priest) were developments
of primitive magic meant to ensure yearly crop growth. By the time
The Golden Bough reached twelve volumes (1911–15), Frazer had

explicitly moved from solving a problem in ancient Roman religion to presenting a general theory about the progress of human thought, based on the comparative method of Smith combined with the evolutionary model of E. B. Tylor's *Primitive Culture* (1871). For Frazer, myths and rituals held the secret of the origins of religion and even science. By assuming that all humans underwent the same stages of development, he tried to use the customs of contemporary tribal people to reconstruct stages in intellectual evolution. (One can detect here echoes of Vico, as well.)

Critics still strive to pin down the genre of Frazer's great work: is it a kind of epic detective story, literary criticism, social science, or, with its shocking (to Victorians) account of savage practices, soft pornography? As anthropology, at any rate, it has prompted many negative judgments: that the comparative method as he practiced it reduced everything to mythical uniformity; that he valued as equal both the trivial observations of travellers and the insights of professionals; that he neglected the precise way in which myth and ritual functioned in the individual local cultures; and that he too easily accepted the notion that religion and myth are a matter of conscious thought. The philosopher Ludwig Wittgenstein noted dryly, "Frazer is much more savage than most of his savages, for these savages will not be so far from any understanding of spiritual matters as an Englishman of the twentieth century." Despite such attacks, the eminent British anthropologist Edward Evans-Pritchard (1902–1973) could still hold that *The Golden Bough* is "an essential source book for all students of human thought."

The 1890 edition of his masterwork saw Frazer at his most ritualistic, stressing the origin of myth from long-forgotten magic practices. While he moved away from the simplicities of this stance over the next decades, ironically, the scholars whose work popularized Frazer among students of Greek myth were most affected by the first edition's bolder views that Frazer himself later abandoned. Between 1900 and 1915, a close-knit group of Classicists in Cambridge (and one Oxford don) applied Frazer's method in a variety of ways to Greek drama, religion, and history. Their work was all the more shocking because they did not start from a Vergilian line only to wander off on ethnological divagations. Instead, they aimed at the main monuments of Greek culture, the Classical art and literature that was widely held at their time to form the absolute standard of high taste and refinement.

The informal "Cambridge School" of interpreters included F. M. Cornford (1874–1943), A. B. Cook (1868–1952), and Gilbert Murray (1866–1957), but it centered around a remarkable woman from Yorkshire, Jane Ellen Harrison (1850–1928) – known to some as Bloody Jane, as she sometimes carried to an extreme the view that Greek myth arose from misunderstood rituals of the most primitive type. (She seems to have been convinced, for instance, that ecstatic followers of Dionysos really did rip apart large wild beasts, as the myths reported.) The skeptical attitude this aroused in some of her British contemporaries is clear from the story that the philosopher Bertrand Russell once promised to buy Harrison a bull if she and her friends would show him how the rite might be accomplished. Harrison declined.

Figure 4.2 Jane Ellen Harrison (1850–1928), pioneering scholar of Greek myth and religion associated with the "Cambridge School" approach to ritual. The portrait by Augustus John (1878–1961) hangs in Newnham College, Cambridge University, where she taught from 1898 to 1922

In her most controlled work, *Prolegomena to the Study of Greek Religion* (1903), Harrison expounded the importance of darker "chthonic" rites within Greek religion: all was not the sweetness and light of the neo-Classic Olympians. *Themis* (1912) shows her extending her range to find in the work of Émile Durkheim (see below) arguments for the crucial role of collective religious activity. Using distinctions found already in late antiquity, she developed the view that myth and ritual were co-equal and co-existent, one being the "thing said" (*legomenon*) while the other was the "thing done" (*dromenon*). More along Frazerian lines, Cornford argued that fifth-century Greek comedy developed from rites for a "year-Daimon" while Murray said the same about tragedy, and Cook, in his multi-volume work on Zeus, speculated about the role of sacral kingship in prehistoric Greece.

The Cambridge School had a curious afterlife in interpretation of myth by Classicists: its excesses nearly killed the ritual approach for half a century, but some of its major insights have now proved durable. Its most important achievement was to have directed attention away from an exclusive focus on canonical, literary versions of myths, towards actual cults and archaeological evidence for belief – still the method used today. While few would argue that myth arises solely as an explanation of no-longer-understood rituals, many scholars of Greek religion acknowledge that they intersected in varied ways. Among those still working in this "ritualist" tradition, Walter Burkert stands out as most interesting, especially in his study *Structure and History in Greek Mythology and Ritual* (1979).

MYTHS AND SOCIETY: FUNCTIONALISTS AND STRUCTURALISTS

The most recent modes of interpreting myths relate them closely to the realities of social life in ancient times. This sort of work grows out of two traditions: one in France that dates its modern beginnings from Émile Durkheim (1858–1917) and his collaborators on the journal *Année sociologique*, the other a "functionalist" position most famously developed by Bronislaw Malinowski (1884–1942), the Polish anthropologist who influenced a generation of scholars through his renowned seminars at the London School of Economics. Durkheim's central ideas – that religion is a symbolic expression, or "collective representation," of underlying social structures, and that there exists a total interdependence of social phenomena in primitive societies – had a great influence on several generations of French classical scholars (as well as on the Englishwoman Jane Harrison). Malinowski, a social anthropologist who felt the powerful influence of J. G. Frazer when young, did intensive fieldwork in the Trobriand Islands of Melanesian New Guinea during the later years of World War I. This experience led to his formulation of a distinctive approach to the role of myth within culture. For him, myth codified the beliefs and morals of a given culture, and was an active force in holding together the social fabric. Myth, wrote Malinowski, was a "charter" for social beliefs.

In the study of actual myths, ancient or modern, the notion of "charter" opens up new perspectives. In the cosmogonic stories of Hesiod's *Theogony*, we can now see that the tales do nothing less than *authorize* a society's gender roles, agricultural practices, familial structures, economic exchanges and legal procedures. What the functional approach does *not* do is explain variety and change within myth systems: why should there be multiple versions of a story within one society if in fact the myths continually prop up social roles that all people acknowledge? Here, more attention has to be given to the innovative power of myth performance. Because stories work with a limited number of symbols and narrative paths, not unlike a language with its finite resources of grammar, any "speaker" can become adept enough to manipulate the system. By making a story, the tribe expresses and even polices itself, true enough; but a sub-group, or even an individual within the society, can gain power in the same way, through myth. (Recall the story in Herodotus, back in Chapter 1, about Pisistratus staging a ride with "Athena.")

The same objection has been brought against "structuralist" interpretations of the working of myth in societies. Two very different, sometimes alarmingly technical methods for studying myths can be traced back to the work of the linguist Ferdinand de Saussure (1857–1913), who taught at Geneva in the early years of the century. Several of his theoretical principles became the foundations of modern structural linguistics. First, Saussure distinguished between two aspects of the "linguistic sign" (roughly, the word): the signifier (i.e. the sequence of sounds which one pronounces – e.g. "dog") and the signified (i.e. the concept to which the word points – e.g.

a canine). The associations are made systematically within a given language: "dog" cannot mean a feline, in English. But what Saussure stressed was the conventional, arbitrary nature of this association between a word and what it "means"; dog, *chien*, *Hund* all refer to the same sort of animal, but each language has developed a different sequence of significant sounds (phonemes) to denote this animal. This insight into the nature of words as conventional signs was important for the development of a larger science of signs, a project already undertaken by the American philosopher C. S. Peirce. In its growth among European scholars, the science of "semiotics" was extended to a range of cultural materials, from culinary habits to the system of fashion and, eventually, to myths. Seen as "coded" messages, mythic tales could thus be explained in such a way that otherwise odd and unique elements fit into place within a system of "signifiers" which made reference to a completely different, inexplicit signified "message." When combined with the new techniques of narratology, as in the work of A. J. Greimas, semiotics thus offered the possibility of systematizing the often wildly various mythic tale-tellings by stripping them down to a series of transformations carried out on significant elements. This seemingly algebraic approach works best with those stories which feature a number of variant versions; in Classical mythology, where we often retain only one or two canonical versions, often literary, of a myth that has been passed down and transmuted by many tellers, the method has met with less success.

Saussure's second major insight, regarding the simultaneous presence of "syntagmatic" and "paradigmatic" levels in language, was crucial for the development of the structural anthropology of Claude Lévi-Strauss. The syntagmatic level is that of linear sequence, the temporal dimension of words coming in a particular order in sentences. It is the axis of combination, along which speakers place items selected to convey their message. The paradigmatic level is the axis of selection, that range of all the available parts of speech in a given category that one could place at any point within a sentence. "I will arise and go now," to take an example, can be rearranged syntagmatically to transmit a different message: "Will I arise and go now?"; obviously, only certain syntagmatic orders carry meaning within English. ("Go I arise now will and" doesn't work.) Paradigmatic, or selectional, changes using different nouns, verbs, and adverbs might produce "You arose and went then" or "He lay down and stayed here." Both axes are at work in the production of any utterance. To interpret any utterance, one has to know the rules of combination and the range of selection.

After doing anthropological fieldwork among Amazonian peoples of Brazil in the 1930s, Lévi-Strauss moved to New York in 1941 to take up a position at the New School for Social Research, where he was later to meet Roman Jakobson (1896–1982), one of the founders of the Prague Linguistic Circle, and an early advocate of Saussurean linguistics. The influence led Lévi-Strauss to write his first structuralist essay, in 1945, for the journal *Word*, in which he applied linguistic principles to other cultural forms. The analogy between human institutions like kinship, and language, became central for his later anthropological work, especially his *Mythologies*, a four-volume study of North American and Amazonian narrative and cultural codes.

The only extended application of his method to Classical mythology came in a 1955 essay on the interpretation of the Oedipus myth. In it, Lévi-Strauss noted that most of the episodes in Theban mythic history can be arranged into a single signifying structure, like a code or analogy, based on central themes. The structure itself comprises two sets of "binary oppositions" (graphically displayed as columns of opposite features) as in Figure 4.3.

"Overvaluation" of kin – Cadmus' obsessive search for his sister or Antigone's decision to die for trying to bury her brother's corpse – is balanced by "undervaluation," as when the sons of Oedipus wage fratricidal war. In the same way, writes Lévi-Strauss, an origin from One (i.e. from the earth, according to the idea of autochthony) is juxtaposed in the myth-complex surrounding Thebes with problematic origins from Two (father and mother). How does one set of oppositions relate to the other? Instead of saying that the myth answers the dilemmas it raises in its symbolic form, Lévi-Strauss stresses that the entire myth (by which he denotes the sum of all versions) attempts to transform one unsolvable problem of origins (where do humans come from – sexual reproduction or out of the earth?) into a more tractable question of social behavior (how should one treat kin?). The *analogous* form that each set of oppositions bears to the other is an assurance, to the society which devised the myth over time, of the essential bond *between* cosmology and society.

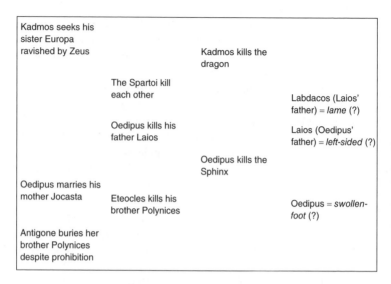

Kadmos seeks his sister Europa ravished by Zeus		Kadmos kills the dragon	
	The Spartoi kill each other		Labdacos (Laios' father) = *lame* (?)
	Oedipus kills his father Laios		Laios (Oedipus' father) = *left-sided* (?)
		Oedipus kills the Sphinx	
Oedipus marries his mother Jocasta	Eteocles kills his brother Polynices		Oedipus = *swollen-foot* (?)
Antigone buries her brother Polynices despite prohibition			

Figure 4.3 Deep structure of the myths of Thebes, as analyzed by French social anthropologist Claude Lévi-Strauss. The first two columns (concerning the status of kin relations) present a mythopoeic transformation of the second pair of columns (concerning the value of autochthony). Myth, in this approach, works as a cognitive tool for re-formulating basic questions of human life

Source: Chart from p. 433 of article "The Structural Study of Myth" by Claude Lévi-Strauss, *Journal of American Folklore* vol. 68 no. 270 (Oct–Dec 1955) 428–44. Published by American Folklore Society. Reproduced with permission.

This rather densely argued incursion into the interpretation of Greek myth has been highly influential. Nevertheless, some object that no single audience of myth-tellers and hearers could have had in mind all the possible paradigmatic variations of the master-myth that Lévi-Strauss envisions. When it comes to classical material, in which only a portion of the entire tale is ever selected for foregrounding in any one work (say, in the play *Oedipus the King*), and where audiences vary widely in space and time, scholars are often less than convinced of the method's usefulness. We need to know, but cannot reconstruct, such simple facts as at what points an ancient audience considered the Oedipus story to have begun and ended.

The structuralist method as practiced by Lévi-Strauss is ultimately best classified along with psychological approaches. Like them, it deduces from one set of surface phenomena in a myth an entirely different underlying "message." In the structuralist analysis, the message has to do with a mediation between binary oppositions relating to important cultural questions – often the oppositions between nature and culture itself. By claiming to interpret myths in this way, Lévi-Strauss is also making assertions about universal cognitive structures of the human mind. He thus opens himself to the same charges of reductionism and over-generalization as were once levelled against Freud's psychoanalytic method. But the richness and variety of the specific individual details with which both men construct their arguments is itself an inviting reason for exploring their work, whether or not one is convinced by the methods at play.

Structuralism was a key inspiration (alongside Durkheimian social analysis) for the work of the so-called Paris School, a group of scholars studying ancient myth in the 1970s and 1980s. Starting from a small core (Pierre Vidal-Naquet, Jean-Pierre Vernant, Nicole Loraux and Marcel Detienne) the informal "school" grew to include dozens of students and associates, whose work has contributed immeasurably to the contemporary understanding of Greek and Roman tales in relation to society. It is difficult to single out one most important work, as topics that have been studied range from Pre-Socratic thought to politics, and sacrificial practices to rhetoric. Two exemplary studies that integrate structural with sociological insights are Vidal-Naquet's analysis of cultivated land in its relation to sacrifice in the *Odyssey*, and Vernant's explication of the goddess Artemis. The former employs the Hesiodic binary distinction between the Gold and Iron ages to explore the range of lands and peoples that Odysseus visits, aligning these in terms of their nearness to either Elysian conditions or cannibalism – which turn out to be quite close to one another. The latter compares the Huntress Artemis with her equally important role as Maiden, concluding that the goddess presides over the borderland between the wild and the civilized, water in terms of landscape or of social life (the transition zone between childhood and maturity). While Vidal-Naquet illuminates the mythic structure and resonances of one epic composition, Vernant ranges over many texts and sources to construct an Artemis that expresses and transcends binary oppositions. His totalizing view, in turn, enables a new appreciation of such myths as the story of Atalantê.

In sum, as a student who embarks on interpreting myths today can choose varieties from within the rich and broad field of structuralist social readings, so, too, she can deploy the resources of other methods – ritualist, psychological, historical and comparative – depending on the types of mythic material that need explication. What works for the story of Atalantê might be irrelevant for Achilles. There is no one best approach to interpretation. Or rather, the best operating procedure is to try out as many relevant methods as possible, and then to articulate the successes and deficiencies of each.

FURTHER READING

The best recent introduction to methods of interpretation is the collection edited by Lowell Edmunds, *Approaches to Greek Myth* (2nd edn, Baltimore: Johns Hopkins University Press, 2014), which contains excellent bibliographies. Eric Csapo, *Theories of Mythology* (Malden: Blackwell, 2005) is a sophisticated, readable explanation of five major traditions. A shorter but useful survey is Fritz Graf's *Greek Mythology: An Introduction* (Baltimore: Johns Hopkins University Press, 1993). The detailed and rich study by Andrew von Hendy, *The Modern Construction of Myth* (Bloomington: Indiana University Press, 2002) traces many connections among myth studies, philosophy, and literary criticism.

The long-lived allegorical method is incisively analyzed by Peter Struck, *Birth of the Symbol: Ancient Readers at the Limits of Their Texts* (Princeton: Princeton University Press 2004). Also informative is Luc Brisson, *How Philosophers Saved Myths* (Chicago: University of Chicago Press, 2004). D. C. Allen, *Mysteriously Meant: The Rediscovery of Pagan Symbolism and Allegorical Interpretation in the Renaissance* (Baltimore: Johns Hopkins University Press, 1971) analyzes later uses of the method.

Christian treatment of some pagan myths is examined by Hugo Rahner, *Greek Myths and Christian Mystery* (New York: Biblo & Tannen, 1971). A fuller overview with good further reading is the essay by Graf, "Myth in Christian Authors," in *A Companion to Greek Mythology*, edited by Ken Dowden and Niall Livingstone (Oxford: Wiley-Blackwell, 2011). On the Middle Ages, see *Classical Myths and Legends in the Middle Ages and Renaissance: A Dictionary* by H. David

Brumble (London: Fitzroy Dearborn, 1998). Of wider scope and detail is the monumental *The Classical Tradition*, edited by Anthony Grafton, Glenn Most, and Salvatore Settis (Cambridge: Harvard University Press, 2010). On the continuing influence of earlier approaches in the early nineteenth century see Anthony Harding, *The Reception of Myth in English Romanticism* (Columbia: University of Missouri Press, 1995).

A lucid application of a modern psychoanalytical approach is by Richard Caldwell, *The Origin of the Gods: A Psychoanalytic Study of Greek Theogonic Myth* (New York: Oxford University Press, 1989). A broad survey can be found in Robert Eisner, *The Road to Daulis: Psychoanalysis, Psychology, and Classical Mythology* (Syracuse: Syracuse University Press, 1987). Otto Rank's *The Myth of the Birth of the Hero* has been reprinted with related essays by Alan Dundes and Lord Raglan in a volume edited by Robert Segal, *In Quest of the Hero* (Princeton: Princeton University Press, 1990).

For investigating the roots of the social and historical methods of interpreting myths, a fine guide is *The Rise of Modern Mythology, 1680–1860*, edited by Burton Feldman and Robert D. Richardson (Bloomington: Indiana University Press, 1972). The social scientific backgrounds are well provided by George W. Stocking in two books, *After Tylor: British Social Anthropology, 1888–1951* (Madison: University of Wisconsin Press, 1995) and *Victorian Anthropology* (New York: Simon and Schuster, 1991). On the key figures, students will want to consult individual biographies and autobiographies from Vico onward. On two pivotal Cambridge scholars, see Robert Ackerman, *J. G. Frazer: His Life and Work* (Cambridge: Cambridge University Press, 1987) and Mary Beard, *The Invention of Jane Harrison* (Cambridge, MA: Harvard University Press, 2002). On the whole movement, see Ackerman's *The Myth and Ritual School: J. G. Frazer and the Cambridge Ritualists* (London: Routledge, 2013). Another intriguing ritual-centered book by Walter Burkert in addition to the volume mentioned in the text is *Homo Necans: The Anthropology of Ancient Greek Sacrificial Ritual and Myth*, trans. P. Bing (Berkeley: University of California Press, 1983).

Ancient forerunners of the historical approach are examined in *The Ancient Concept of Progress and Other Essays on Greek Literature and Belief* by Eric Robertson Dodds (New York: Oxford University Press, 1973). Texts of the Sophists are translated in John Dillon (ed.),

The Greek Sophists (London: Penguin, 2003) and of the Pre-Socratics in Jonathan Barnes (ed.), *Early Greek Philosophy* (London: Penguin, 2001).

The best starting point for further study of Lévi-Strauss is by his fellow anthropologist, Edmund Leach, *Claude Lévi-Strauss* (Chicago: University of Chicago Press, 1989). The essay mentioned in the text is "The Structural Study of Myth," in *Structural Anthropology* (Garden City, NY: Doubleday/Anchor, 1955: 202–28). For samples of Malinowski's method, see *Argonauts of the Western Pacific* (Routledge: London, 1922) and *Magic, Science, Religion, and Other Essays* (New York: Free Press 1948). R. L. Gordon, *Myth, Religion, and Society* (Cambridge: Cambridge University Press, 1981) is a very good collection introducing the work of the Paris School, with full bibliography.

Two Americans have been brilliant expositors of the method: Charles Segal, *Tragedy and Civilization: An Interpretation of Sophocles* (Cambridge, MA: Harvard University Press, 1981) and Froma Zeitlin, *Playing the Other* (Chicago: University of Chicago Press, 1995). She has also edited shorter works of J.-P. Vernant in translation, *Mortals and Immortals: Collected Essays* (Princeton: Princeton University Press, 1991).

5

MYTHS, MEDIA, MEMORIES

Myths do not swim on land. To be less Delphic: myths need a medium in which to survive, as much as do (almost all) fish (mud-skippers excepted). Even in the ancient world, myths came already packaged in literary or subliterary verbal genres (epics, folktales, anecdotes, jokes). Or, they inhabited other artistic forms, from vase-paintings to architectural features such as temple pediments. This chapter presents a condensed overview, first, of a key factor in the transformation and transmission of myths: their Roman reception. Then, we turn to sample the wide spectrum of media through which myths have been transmitted and reshaped.

ROMAN RECEPTION OF MYTH

This book thus far has intentionally focused on the sources of mythology in ancient Greece. What about that other major civilization of the ancient Mediterranean that we are in the habit of calling Classical? (Egypt, Anatolia, and the Near East did not make it into the "Classical" club in the West's narrative of its cultural affiliations – another story.) Didn't the people of ancient Italy have myths as well?

The answer is complicated and deserves a book of its own. But a brief overview is worthwhile. To begin with, we should be careful to speak about *peoples* of ancient Italy, about most of whom we know very little. Before the rise of Rome in approximately the eighth century BC, and well into the days of the city's zenith, there were dozens of languages and dialects spoken in Italy. Some were related to Latin (strictly, the dialect of the tribal group settled around Rome's seven hills). Speakers of Oscan and Umbrian had their own religious vocabulary and rituals, related to Roman but distinct. We do not have their myths, although it is a good bet that they influenced the stories of their more powerful neighbor. In addition, Celtic speakers dwelt in the northern part of the Italian peninsula; indigenous peoples of Sicily had their own culture and languages; speakers of Punic, the Semitic language of the Carthaginians of North Africa (ultimately from Phoenicia) have left inscriptions in Sardinia and Sicily; southern Italy was essentially an extension of Greek culture through early colonization (Magna Graecia – "Great Greece" as it was called). And there was the highly advanced civilization of the mysterious Etruscans.

Although we possess thousands of short Etruscan inscriptions, spanning nearly eight hundred years starting around 700 BC, on dedicated offerings, paintings and other objects, they are largely undecipherable. (Etruscan is not thought to be related to any other surviving tongue, although the alphabet is basically Greek.) Furthermore, we have no longer narrative text. So we cannot tell what tales the inhabitants of central Italy, to whom the Romans attributed much of their own technical lore and religious practices, might have been composing about their own gods and heroes. The lack of readable texts is especially frustrating for students of myth since even the Greeks considered the Etruscans to be a very ancient people, either "Pelasgians" (the pre-Greek inhabitants of the Aegean) or refugees from the once flourishing civilization of Lydia. Bound by trade networks with other cultures throughout Europe, the Etruscans in the sixth century especially were importers of Greek goods. From Etruscan pottery and wall paintings we can see that Greek religious figures were being blended with their own native gods. "Apulu" (borrowed from Apollo) was treated as a death-demon and "Artumes" (his sister Artemis) as a fertility goddess. "Menerva" was, as in the Roman pantheon (as "Minerva"), equivalent to Athena, but in Etruscan depictions, a controller of lightning.

A much later source, filtered through Roman writings, summarizes the Etruscan creation story, in which a god creates the universe in the course of 12,000 years, with the human race arriving only halfway through this period (*Suda*, tenth century AD). Recalling a trace element of another myth, Cicero said that the Etruscan knowledge of divination and related lore came to them from a preternaturally wise child, Tages, who sprang from recently ploughed earth (Cic. *Divinatione* 2.50). His esoteric teaching seems to have included how to found cities and apportion land, as well as how to know the will of the gods through signs detected in weather, animal entrails, and the flight of birds. Long contact between Romans and Etruscans either produced, or at least allowed them to perceive, similarities in their respective divinities: for instance, the Etruscan sky god Tinia equates with Jupiter, Uni with Juno, and the water divinity Neθuns with Neptune (two words probably linguistically related).

Exactly the same process of making equations among members of the pantheon occurred when Roman culture encountered Greek. This in turn brings us to the problematic search for truly *Roman* myth. Romans venerated dozens of divinities about whom we have no connected narratives, from Consus (god of storage) to Faunus (wild nature), and Janus (god of doorways – from which we have both "January" and "janitor"). In everyday life, such gods of hearth and home were probably as important as the "major" divinities we recognize (mostly guided by our perception of the Greek situation). Paired with the Olympian set of Twelve Gods, the following Roman figures were considered (roughly) the same: Jupiter (Zeus), Juno (Hera), Minerva (Athena), Venus (Aphrodite), Mars (Ares), Mercury (Hermes), Neptune (Poseidon), Pluto (Hades), Ceres (Demeter), Diana (Artemis), Vulcan (Hephaestus), and Liber (Dionysos). But while the names differ, it is difficult to discover myths about any one of these that are not somehow simply taken over from Greek sources. As for the beliefs and rituals associated with the gods, surface similarities to Greek equivalents soon vanish once one looks a bit more deeply, as can be seen, for instance, from the examples of Jupiter and his wife Juno. Her connection with marriage and birth is at first sight like Hera's. But Juno herself (under the name "Lucina" – "who brings to light") is the one invoked at Rome to ensure successful delivery, whereas in Greek it is the function of her *daughter* Eileithuia (as in Hesiod, *Theog.* 291). What is more, Juno in Roman cult seems to have a connection with the rearing of young men, as an armed warrior goddess – a function most clearly associated with Athena on the Greek side.

Jupiter, too, cannot be viewed as an exact duplicate of Zeus. In worship as opposed to myths distinctive Roman traits emerge. Though associated with phenomena of the sky – rain, lightning – he is also tied to places where the augurs, experts in bird divination, took their sightings. Like Zeus, he has a political function, especially under the form Optimus Maximus, and was associated with victory in battle. Yet he also is bound up with the making of wine through such festivals as the *Visalia rustica* at the beginning of the vintage. In Greek cult, these are areas reserved for Dionysos, son of Zeus. As with his wife, the treatment of Jupiter reflects a separately elaborated, independent cultural tradition. Yet, as we shall see shortly, Jupiter is actually one of the few gods who can claim the same origins as his Greek equivalent.

What, then, were the myths that we might classify as Roman as opposed to Greek borrowings? The question takes us back to what we believe the term "myth" might mean. If we insist on stories about the doings of divinities, then Roman "myths" are thin on the ground. But if we expand our scope to include legendary heroes, city-founders and saviors of the people, Rome is as rich in tales as any city-state in Greece. (It helps to remember, too, that until its expansion in the fourth century BC, Rome *was* essentially just another large city-state.) One simply has to get accustomed to reading "myth" in what the Romans treated as their national history. The key sources for this are the first books of the history by Livy (59 BC–AD 17) and the *Roman Antiquities* by Dionysius of Halicarnassus (c. 60 BC–7 BC), a Greek writer long resident in Rome. The latter, especially, was not just keen to show that the area around Rome had been first colonized by Greeks from Arcadia (and that Latin was mostly a Greek dialect!). He was also an interpreter in the popular rationalist mode (on which see the Chapter 4). The twins Romulus and Remus, eventual founders of Rome, had as infants been exposed to starve, but were suckled by a she-wolf – so the traditional tale went. But Dionysius much prefers the common-sense explanation that it was a former prostitute nicknamed "She Wolf" (Lupa) who fed and raised them (Bk. 1.84). With this authorial attitude, fantastic or mythical narrative elements were bound to be rooted out.

This is not the place to rehearse the highlights of Roman "myth-istory." It is worth mentioning, however, why scholars hesitate to accept the legends, at least as found in Livy and other writers, as at all factual. In Chapter 2 we had occasion to refer to the idea of "comparative mythology," an offshoot of comparative historical linguistics. Divine names, as was pointed out, are among the shared vocabulary in the daughter tongues descending from an original "Indo-European" linguistic super-group. Roman "Jupiter" is reconstructed as coming from *Dieu-pater, "sky father"; compare the Greek phrase Zeus pater "Zeus-father." Such relics must be evidence for a once common Indo-European religion. Based on texts in Latin, Greek, Sanskrit, Hittite and other older Indo-European languages, scholars can also reconstruct shared stories about gods and heroes – that is to say, Indo-European "myths."

In the twentieth century, the French scholar Georges Dumézil (1898–1986) produced numerous studies in comparative mythology, introducing the neglected evidence of myths from the Caucasus region, particularly from Ossetic, a language descended from the Indo-Iranian subgroup of Indo-European. Dumézil was a student of Marcel Mauss and Marcel Granet, two associates of Émile Durkheim (see Chapter 4). He thus brought to the study of myths a much more sophisticated theoretical outlook than had been available in the previous century. Dumézil's detailed equations among mythic motifs in Irish, Germanic, Roman, and associated traditions demonstrated that Indo-European myths embody a specific *social ideology*. As for Malinowski and the followers of Durkheim, myth for him represents one strand in a tightly knit web that undergirds social institutions. Beneath the Roman historical accounts, Dumézil perceived a much older Indo-European ideology built on the notion that three "functions" make up society: sovereignty; military strength; and agricultural abundance, corresponding to classes of sacred kings; warriors; and the common people. The worship of Jupiter, Mars, and Quirinus (the protector of the citizenry) was marked at Rome by the existence of a special priest (the *flamen*) devoted to each of these three major gods.

With the tripartite structure in mind, Dumézil explained the mythic background for the legendary war between Rome and the rich Sabine people, in which Romulus (a son of Mars) with accomplices abducted Sabine women to be their wives. He saw in the reconciliation with the Sabine king Titus Tatius a mythic expression of the "third function" being incorporated into Rome's pre-existing other two. Numa Pompilius, the second king according to Roman "history," was revealed to have close mythical cousins in Ireland, Scythia, and ancient Iran. Another figure in Livy's account, the hero Horatius Cocles, behaves like the Irish warrior Cú Chulainn and the Scandinavian Egill. Even the historical figure Camillus, defender of Rome against the Gauls (c. 446–365 BC), fits the template of a mythical hero associated with the Indo-European dawn goddess. In parallel with his excavation of these myths, Dumézil pointed out inherited ancient Indic parallels that can explain a number of otherwise enigmatic features in such Roman rituals as the sacrifice of the "October Horse."

At Rome, then, the categories of myth and legend had been absorbed into a secularized heroic history, while religious practice was less bound up with explanatory tales than seems to have been the case in Greek city-states. We can understand, therefore, how the exotic myth-laden genres of epic, drama, and lyric song ignited the Roman imagination. Through them, Rome became the first "receptor" of the mythic inheritance, and Latin writers the first to take on massive translation from the Greek. It was almost exclusively through Roman intermediaries that myths reached later western Europe and eventually the rest of the world. Ovid and Vergil, two authors of the Augustan period (c. 35 BC–AD 14), proved to be enormously influential.

It is not easy to summarize how elegantly and completely these Latin writers transform Greek myths and adapt them into their own literary and social worlds. Many scholarly books have been devoted in the past half-century to what has been called "the allusive art." For the reader who knows the source text or tradition – as most of the elite audience at Rome would – there is a sustained pleasure in recognizing deft allusions, slightly changed similes, or a new take on an old character. For some who could read Greek as well as Latin, Vergil and his compatriots offered yet another level of interest, making bilingual puns. Latin poets were devoted to the techniques of the Alexandrian writers, a group of third- and second-century BC Greek scholar-authors who enjoyed the patronage of Alexander's royal successors in the Egyptian city he had founded. For such poets as Callimachus (c. 310–240 BC), the ideal work was compact but dense; episodic; using odd lore or arcane versions; seemingly casual and small-voiced (unlike bombastic epic); but immensely learned. The Roman imitators managed to perfect this style.

One example, out of hundreds, can give at least a taste of these Roman creative transmutations. Ovid was the supreme re-shaper of Greek myth. His *Metamorphoses* (c. 8 BC) presents in fifteen chapters more than 250 individual mythic stories forming a continuous narrative that starts with the beginnings of the world. Digressive tales-within-tales make the book into a labyrinthine house of mirrors, one story reflecting others, audiences and tellers interchanged in dizzying speed. Ovid's sources included earlier collections of transformation tales, now lost, like the *Ornithogonia* by Boios, a third-century BC poem about humans who changed into birds. Some of his sources survive, allowing comparisons. To Ovid's narrative in Book Three (lines 528–733) of the death of Pentheus, king of Thebes, we can juxtapose Euripides' final tragedy, the *Bacchae* (405 BC). The drama presents the arrival in Thebes of an alluring androgynous figure – Dionysos in disguise – who has come to take vengeance for the treatment of his mother Semele, now dead. She had been mocked by the citizens when claiming to be pregnant by Zeus (whose lightning ultimately incinerated her). Dionysos brings his ecstatic rites to the city, driving its women to the mountains where they joyously dance and drink. Pentheus, the moralistic king, vows to eradicate the new religion, but is lured by the disguised Dionysos into voyeuristically observing the worshipers of the god (the Bacchae). Glimpsed by the women, who become frenzied, he is torn limb from limb. (All of this is described in a vivid messenger speech, after which Pentheus' own mother, hallucinating that she has killed a lion, carries his head on stage.)

Ovid brilliantly handles the self-imposed challenge of condensing the 1,400-line play – originally a mix of speech, dance, and music – into two hundred lines of Latin hexameter verse. Lacking the device of the Euripidean dramatic prologue, in which the newly arrived god discloses his plan to the audience, Ovid introduces his Pentheus as mocking the famous Tiresias. The blind seer prophesies that Pentheus, failing to worship the approaching god Bacchus (in Greek, Dionysos), will be torn asunder. In other words, Ovid gives away the dramatic ending before the action has even begun. But of course, his learned audience of readers at Rome already *knew* the way the tragedy unfolds; the plot is not what they are interested in, but rather the compact and elegant handling of the centuries-old Greek play. In the drama, Pentheus threatens a crackdown, speaking only to Tiresias,

his grandfather Cadmus, and the chorus of women who have travelled from Asia with the disguised stranger. But in Ovid's version,
the Theban king delivers a Roman political speech to the entire
citizenry of Thebes, decrying their unmartial decadence and taste
for foreign deities (two very real concerns of the Emperor Augustus,
Ovid's patron). The cleverest Ovidian bit comes in his pausing the
dramatic sequence, just before the abrupt downfall of Pentheus. A
captured servant of Bacchus, "Acoetes," tells Pentheus a long story
about escaping after his ship was miraculously transformed into a
floating vineyard by a youth he and his crewmates had captured on
the way from Chios to Naxos. Only Acoetes resisted the crew's plan
to ransom the beautiful young man – so he alone is not turned into a
dolphin by the disguised god. Or is this Acoetes the *same* god in new
disguise? Ovid cunningly leaves it open. The finale comes in a rush:
an enraged Pentheus dashes off to the woods, where his mother and
aunts, despite his piteous pleas, dismember him (this time thinking
he is a boar), and the episode fades into a laconic religious conclusion: now warned, the women of Thebes "celebrate the novel rites"
(*nova sacra frequentant*) dedicating frankincense on sacred altars.

MYTHIC MEDIA: FROM ANCIENT TO MODERN

Just listing the works that have transmitted, re-shaped or been influenced by Classical myth amounts to surveying almost all Western
culture since antiquity. The *Oxford Guide to Classical Mythology in the
Arts, 1300–1990s* takes two volumes and more than 1,300 pages simply to catalogue works and their creators (while leaving out another
thousand years of the story). Exhaustive surveys of the reception of
nearly every Classical author are now available, thanks to a steady
growth in scholarly interest over the last few decades. In the limited
scope of this volume, I can provide only a bird's-eye view of the
modes in which mythology has been handled since ancient times,
and the media that continue to rely on it for inspiration.

PROSE

As most ancient Greek and Latin treatments of myth were poetic,
telling the tales in prose involved several larger shifts in attitude. In
the late sixth century BC in Greece, writing in prose rather than

traditional poetic style was a bold move that also proclaimed a conscious challenge to the elite. Fables of Aesop seem to have been the inspiration for some first attempts. Herodotus, the first complete surviving prose author, transmits myths and folktales, but, as we have seen in earlier chapters, also takes a critical attitude toward them. To accept the Homeric version of "history" was to invest in epic notions of heroism and aristocratic power. Prose could be a tool for questioning these.

The Herodotean model for narrating complicated tales from exotic lands, as *historiê* (literally "research") inspired later Greek imaginative prose. Daphnis and Chloe by Longus transforms a bucolic love story into a myth of its own. Set on Sappho's island of Lesbos, but some 800 years after the poetess, it tells how the beautiful young couple of the title, as yet innocent of sex, undergo attacks by pirates, near-rapes, and a joyous final recognition (based on tokens of identity, as in folktales and Euripidean drama). The god Pan intervenes as savior, and the whole story is framed as a *muthos* created by Eros. We are reminded that *muthos*, already by the time of Aristotle in the fourth century BC, could be used to mean simply "plot" – but this is a plot involving all the elements that we associate with stories of gods and heroes. In effect, myth is re-imagined in terms of everyday human experiences. In various ways, the surviving Greek and Roman novels (by Heliodorus, Achilles Tatius, Petronius, and Apuleius among others) employ the same method, borrowing freely from mythic motifs and their earlier use in epic and drama to craft stories about mortal adventures, sometimes to ironic effect. This strategy for incorporating myth while not using the well-known figures of ancient story has persisted to the present day.

The Middle Ages saw the continued production of prose-handbooks and encyclopedias summarizing and explaining myths, by such authors as Fulgentius, Isidore of Seville, and anonymous commentators on the ever-popular Vergil and Ovid. Much of this work was for teaching young students. But it was also a time of creative reworking of ancient tales, radically adapted rather than translated verbatim from the originals. Medieval Ireland offers an interesting example. While possessing its own native saga tradition in such works as *The Cattle Raid of Cooley* (c. AD 1100), by the end of the eleventh century, the Irish had produced several prose versions of the *Fall of Troy* attributed to the sixth-century AD writer Dares Phrygius; a book of lore about Alexander the Great; a prose version of Vergil, called *Adventures of Aeneas* (*Imtheachta Aeniasa*); and renditions, again in prose, of Latin poems such as Lucan's *Pharsalia* and the *Thebaid* of Statius. Most surprising, some anonymous Irish writer created a wonderful ten-page mini-version of the Homeric *Odyssey*, the *Going Astray of Ulysses Son of Laertes*.

The long and rich history of the modern novel, reaching back to the seventeenth century, was shaped much more by a reaction against medieval romances of the Arthurian type – which were in turn analogous to heroic sagas from antiquity, if not directly influenced by them. Classical myth, when alluded to by a novelist like Henry Fielding (in *Tom Jones* and *Joseph Andrews*) marks the narrator as an informed man of taste but ends up mangled or ironically inappropriate in the mouths of his less educated characters. In *Middlemarch* (1872) by George Eliot (Mary Ann Evans) the unattractive Rev. Casaubon is a pedant with ambitions to write *The Key to All Mythologies*. Because of its elite associations, in general the Classical world and its mythic heritage is held at arm's length by popular prose fiction. But in the late nineteenth and early twentieth centuries this attitude shifted. The French writer Émile Zola acknowledged the influence of the ancient *Daphnis and Chloe* on his *Fortune of the Rougons* (1871) about an extended mid-nineteenth-century family. André Gide (1869–1951) used the technique of imagining the thoughts and adventures of Greek mythic characters whether plunged into the modern day, as in *Prometheus Ill-Bound* (1899), where the Titan exchanges his Caucasian rock for a Parisian cafe, or *Theseus* (1946) a meditative retrospective by the aging slayer of the Minotaur. Most famously, James Joyce in *Ulysses* re-cast the epic return of Odysseus as a single day that intertwines the lives of a Jewish Dubliner, Leopold Bloom, and a young aesthete, the mythically named Stephen Dedalus (like his namesake, a cunning artisan). Joyce's "mythical method" of making parallels with antiquity represented, in the admiring view of the poet T. S. Eliot, a way to order contemporary chaos, "a step toward making the modern world possible for art."

Science fiction has become the modern prose form that most takes advantage of Classical myths. The method of projecting into the future the social institutions and tales of a re-imagined alien past can be seen already in forerunners such as *Seven Days in New Crete* (1949) about a futuristic world in which people worship a Triple Goddess. Not accidentally its author was Robert Graves, a translator and popularizer of myth who had published a short time before his idiosyncratic book *The White Goddess*, which he dubbed "an historical grammar of the language of poetic myth." At one end of the spectrum are young-adult fantasies, like *Fool's Run* (1987) by Patricia McKillip which re-imagines the Orpheus myth with a beautiful female musician as protagonist, whose twin sister has been imprisoned in an orbiting underworld. More ambitious is the cycle *Ilium* and *Olympos* (2004, 2005) by Dan Simmons. In a highly literary pastiche it re-stages the plot of the *Iliad* as a future experiment manipulated by post-human "god" directors. and observed by a time-traveling Homerist. Although we may think of sci-fi as a recent invention, its roots go back to antiquity, when Lucian of Samosata (second century AD) wrote his *True History* about moon-dwellers and wars in space. The best candidate for its modern progenitor is *Frankenstein* (1818), written by Mary Shelley and bearing the significant subtitle: *The Modern Prometheus*.

POETRY

Mary Shelley's poet husband Percy Bysshe Shelley provides a fine example of the reception of Greek myth by the all-important Romantics, in dialogue with ancient models while looking forward to modern treatments. Although his four-act *Prometheus Unbound* takes the form of drama, it encapsulates a tradition, common since the end of antiquity, of reading rather than performing Greek tragedy. In effect it is a long poem rather than an actable play. Only in the nineteenth century did the re-performance of Greek and Roman plays as actual dramatic pieces begin (see the section on Drama below).

Written during the same period that his wife was composing her Promethean novel, the play by Shelley presents its title character as the ideal Romantic hero – a rebel adamantly against authority, who remains unreconciled to Jupiter, and is finally released not (as in the ancient myth) by Heracles' intervention but because his oppressor loses political power. "The moral interest of the fable, which is so powerfully sustained by the sufferings and endurance of Prometheus, would be annihilated if we could conceive of him as unsaying his high language and quailing before his successful and perfidious adversary," wrote Shelley. This revolutionary attitude expressed itself in his dramatic poem *Hellas* about the War of Greek Independence (the conflict that also inspired, and led to the death of, Shelley's friend the poet Byron).

From late antiquity onward, epic poems were the privileged form of reception for Classical myths. Alongside the re-copying and explication of the epics of Homer, Vergil, Ovid, and Statius, new epics were produced in a mythic form. For example, the *Psychomachia* ("Soul Battle") of Prudentius (c. AD 348–410) depicted in Vergilian style an allegorical war between vices and virtues (e.g. Chastity and Lust), with a Christian as ultimate hero. Two great poets of the fourteenth century, Dante and Chaucer, devised episodic poems of epic length (*The Divine Comedy* and *The Canterbury Tales*), both of them deeply influenced by Ovid and Vergil, even though their main purpose is not to display Classical myths. Dante's tour of Hell (with Vergil as his guide) features a number of men or monsters familiar from the *Metamorphoses*, but he is not a slavish imitator of the Roman poet. In the Eighth Circle the poet glimpses a horrible two-way transformation (man to snake and vice versa) that outdoes anything in the *Metamorphoses*. He apostrophizes the older poet:

> Be silent Ovid, of Cadmus and Arethusa;
>
> For if him to a snake, her to a fountain,
>
> Converts he fabling, that I grudge him not;
>
> Because two natures never front to front
>
> Has he transmuted, so that both the forms
>
> To interchange their matter ready were.
>
> (*Inferno* 25.97–12, trans. H. W. Longfellow)

The epic *Faerie Queen* by Edmund Spenser (1590–96) and *Paradise Lost* by John Milton (1667) would be unthinkable without models of how Classical epic handled myth, although the latter relies on the Bible and the former on medieval romances for its immediate subject-matter.

Lyric poetry in Greece was tightly bound to the celebration of gods and heroes, whether in hymns, dithyrambs, or praise-poems. Medieval poets continued to write imitations of this poetry. The so-called Wandering Scholars, footloose university students of the twelfth and thirteenth century, are credited with a collection of about 200 short lyric pieces that goes by the name *Carmina Burana* (after the southern Bavarian monastery of Benediktbeuern where a manuscript containing them was rediscovered in 1803). These use names and figures from Classical myth, such as "Fortuna," as decoration. Several of the collection were set to music by the German composer Carl Orff (1895–1982). From the Renaissance to the Romantic period, odes built on a Classical template and often filled with mythic allusions were in vogue. Abraham Cowley's *Ode on the Restoration of Charles II* (1660) poses itself as inferior to the epic treatment that his king deserves:

> Did I not know my humble verse must be
> But ill-proportion'd to the height of thee
> Thou and the world should see
> How much my Muse the foe of flattery,
> Does make true Praise her Labour and Design,
> An *Iliad* or an *Aeneid* should be Thine.

This sort of overblown rhetoric eventually led to a reaction. But the use of Classical myth as a subject increased, if anything, in the late nineteenth and twentieth centuries. In fact, it might be said that the Modernists of the early twentieth century re-captured the true force of mythic allusion. *The Waste Land* of T. S. Eliot (1922 – the same year as Joyce's *Ulysses*) embeds the myth of Philomela and Procne (see Chapter 1), perhaps ironically glancing at two recent reworkings (Oscar Wilde's 1881 *The Burden of Itys* and Algernon Swinburne's 1904 *Itylus*). The list of lyric poets composing about, or even in the voice of, ancient mythic characters is long. It includes such notable writers as Ezra Pound, W. H. Auden, Osip Mandelstam, Seamus Heaney, D. H. Lawrence, Robert Frost, and Jorie Graham. Modern Greek poets, in particular, have created a remarkable series of re-imaginings of their own ancient stories, especially George Seferis,

Constantine Cavafy, and Yannis Ritsos. Sometimes poets make explicit their debt to particular ancient versions, as in the emotionally complex refashionings by the British writer Ted Hughes titled *Tales from Ovid* (1997).

DRAMA

In 1999 a dramatic adaptation of Hughes' *Tales* was staged in Shakespeare's hometown, Stratford-upon-Avon. At the time, it was pointed out how appropriate this was. Shakespeare as a schoolboy learned his Ovid almost on the very spot, as part of his "smalle Latin and lesse Greek" (actually, a considerable amount by our standards). He clearly recalled his reading of the *Metamorphoses* when writing *Romeo and Juliet*, a close analogue for the tale of Pyramus and Thisbe (*Met.* Book IV). In *The Tempest*, the speech in which Prospero gives up his powers is closely modeled on an incantatory speech by Medea in the *Metamorphoses* (Bk. VII, 179–233). Shakespeare's familiarity with Roman history is of course well known (*Julius Caesar*, *Coriolanus*). His less often produced *Troilus and Cressida*, however, can claim deeper mythic roots, going back to the archaic Greek Cyclic epics, then growing through a fifth-century play by Sophocles (*Troilus*, now lost); the *Story of Troy's Fall* by Dares (sixth century AD); Chaucer's *Troilus and Criseyde* (c. 1385); and Robert Henryson's fifteenth-century narrative in Scots dialect, *The Testament of Cresseid*.

Modern theater would be poorer without the myth-inspired works of such twentieth-century French playwrights as Jean-Paul Sartre (*The Flies*, 1943, a version of the Electra myth); Jean Giraudoux (*Electra* 1937); Jean Cocteau (*Antigone*, 1922; *The Infernal Machine*, about Oedipus, 1934) and Jean Anouilh (*Medea*, 1946). The technique of transposing ancient myth to the contemporary urban scene runs through them, while wartime suffering and existentialist philosophical ideas lie beneath their surface. The influence of Friedrich Nietzsche's manifesto, *The Birth of Tragedy out of the Spirit of Music* (1872), with its opposition of Apolline and Dionysian ways of being, is clear. In Anglo-American theater, the "mythic method" was employed with similar jarring effect in Tennessee Williams' 1957 play *Orpheus Descending*, about the erotically charged arrival in a Southern town of a young guitar-strumming hero (played by Marlon Brando in the 1959 film version). Eugene O' Neill's three-play cycle *Mourning Becomes Electra*, based on the *Oresteia* trilogy of Aeschylus, sets the story of Agamemnon and his revenge-wracked family in New England during the Civil War period. The tale of the House of Atreus also provided the basic plot for *The Family Reunion* (1939), a verse drama by T. S. Eliot about a problematic English upper-class family, which featured the (not especially successful) devices of minor characters who comment like a Greek chorus and a major character apparently pursued by the Furies.

The creation of plays on ancient themes, and the generalized habit of alluding to Classical myths were common already in the Renaissance and early modern periods. The French dramatist Robert Garnier, for instance, produced an *Hippolytus* in 1573 and an *Antigone* in 1580, the latter padded out with scenes from works by Seneca and Statius. French "Classical" theater was created by two dramatists of the next century, Pierre Corneille and Jean Racine, prolific inventors of myth-themed plays. But regular public re-performance of ancient drama in Greek, Latin, or the European vernacular languages hardly occurred from the sixth century AD until some tentative revivals in early nineteenth-century Germany (e.g. August Schlegel's *Ion* of 1802). By mid-century, translated plays of all three major ancient tragedians could be seen in London and Paris. Cambridge University staged its first full production of a play in Greek (*Ajax* by Sophocles) in 1882 (and the tradition continues today). By the early twentieth century the trickle had turned into a flood; every decade since then has seen a leap in the number of ancient plays re-enacted. Festivals like that organized at Delphi, Greece by the poet Angelos Sikelianos and his wife Eva Palmer (inspired by the opera festival that Richard Wagner [1813–1883] inaugurated at Bayreuth in 1876) introduced mythic dramas to thousands starting in the 1930s. Similar efforts have been highly successful in Syracuse, Sicily and Epidaurus in Greece. In New York alone, within a single season (1998–99), theatergoers could attend a *Medea* by the National Theater of Greece; *Oedipus the King*; the experimental *Fragments of a Greek Trilogy* by Andrei Serban (original 1974) and a blend of two Euripidean tragedies in the *Iphigeneia Cycle* by JoAnne Akalaitis, who went on to do versions of *Antigone* (2012) and *The Bacchae* (2009), the latter with the composer Philip Glass. Full details about thousands of modern productions can be found at the Archive of Performances of Greek and Roman Drama, based at Oxford University (www.apgrd.ox.ac.uk).

MUSIC

In composing music for modern performance of an ancient Greek tragedy, Philip Glass followed in the footsteps of such earlier figures as Felix Mendelssohn, who wrote an overture and seven choruses for an 1841 staging of *Antigone* for the Prussian court in Potsdam. Another Sophoclean play, *Oedipus Rex*, was transformed into an opera–oratorio by Igor Stravinsky, with a libretto by the ubiquitous Jean Cocteau (translated into Latin and first performed in 1927). Unlike drama and the verbal arts already mentioned, music is itself a *mythologized* creative medium. That is to say, the old stories talked about characters involved in the art. Apollo was celebrated as leader of the Muses and a virtuoso player of the concert-style *kithara* (ancestor of the modern guitar). Hermes invented the smaller, softer-sounding lyre. Athena first discovered the music of the double-pipe (*aulos* in Greek) but threw it away because it distorted her face when she played; the satyr Marsyas who picked it up and became an expert piper later lost a musical challenge to Apollo, for which he paid with his skin. And, most notoriously, Orpheus, the singer who could enchant animals and move trees with his music, succeeded through his songs in persuading the gods of the underworld to let him lead from Hades his recently deceased wife Eurydice – only to lose her once more when he broke a taboo and glanced back to ensure that she was following.

Inevitably, the story of Orpheus became the single most favored inspiration for musical treatment. The genre of opera originated with re-imaginings of the Thracian hero's story and an attempt to re-create the format of fifth-century drama. Jacopo Peri's *L'Euridice*, first performed in the Palazzo Pitti, Florence in October 1600, kept the tone of earlier bucolic plays by substituting a happy ending. A darker ending marks Claudio Monteverdi's *L'Orfeo* (1607) with Orpheus forced to evade the worshipers of Bacchus who would tear him apart. The seventeenth century saw operatic versions by Luigi Rossi (1647) and Antonio Sartorio (1672). Christoph Gluck's *Orfeo ed Euridice*, first staged in 1762, played to the sentiment of his age with a Eurydice revived by Love, then celebrated in the final chorus "*Trionfi Amore!*" ("Let love be triumphant!"). Because it became so well known, Gluck's version lent itself all the more to parody in the next century by Jacques Offenbach in his comic opera *Orpheus in the Underworld* (premiered 1858), complete with "can-can" dancers in its "Infernal Galop" (Act 2, Scene 2).

Almost every other musical genre has mined the resources of Classical myth, although less obsessively than opera. A sampling from the twentieth century alone includes Benjamin Britten's orchestral work *Young Apollo* (1939); his haunting solo oboe piece *Six Metamorphoses after Ovid* (1951); and his last vocal work *Phaedra* (1975); Harry Partch's *Ulysses at the Edge of the World* (1955); incidental music for Aeschylus' *Oresteia*, by Pierre Boulez (1945); Elliott Carter's incidental music for *Philoctetes* (1936) and Egon Wellesz's many compositions to accompany stage productions, such as *Alcestis* (1924), and *The Bacchae* (1931). The contemporary composer Harrison Birtwistle has focused on the Orpheus theme in running the gamut of musical genres, with *Nenia: The Death of Orpheus* (1970), a work for soprano and chamber ensemble, the cycle *Orpheus Elegies* (2004) – responding to Rainer Maria Rilke's *Sonnets to Orpheus* (1922) – and his memorable 1994 opera, *The Second Mrs. Kong*, a surreal mélange in which the young model for Vermeer's painting *Girl with a Pearl Earring* is pursued by the 1930s film monster King Kong with the help of the archaic Greek musician, whose head keeps singing despite his later decapitation (a detail that alludes to an actual ancient version).

In an era of mashups where "popular" music and Classical motifs increasingly intertwine, a YouTube browser can discover the satirical cantata *Iphigenia in Brooklyn* (1970s) by Peter Schickele ("P. D. Q. Bach"), next to "Tales of Brave Ulysses" by the rock group Cream, and a hip-hop adaptation of Aeschylus' tragedy about the Theban war, Will Power's *The Seven*, with a DJ acting as typical Greek chorus and music ranging from gospel to doo-wop – all hatched from Classical myths.

DANCE

Just as the musical reception of myth could look to legendary ancient performers, so dance had its role model in Apollo, "Leader of the Muses." A now famous ballet with that title premiered in 1928, with music by Igor Stravinsky, choreographed by George Balanchine, then just twenty-four years old. Both men later noted that in part *their* model had been the thirteen-hour-long *Ballet of the Night* of

1653. At that nearly mythical performance the French monarch Louis XIV, a semi-professional dancer, himself played an Apollo-like role as self-styled "sun king," with his court circling around like planets, in a grand finale timed to coincide with sunrise. And if we trace *that* performance model back far enough, the ancient roots of myth-themed ballet appear in the long-lived form of "pantomime dance," an art form of the Roman Empire, hugely popular from the first through sixth centuries AD. A dancer, most often solo, who "imitates all things" (the literal meaning of *panto-mimos*) performed this genre, masked and in elegant costume, at public events like musical contests or in private settings. The topics were most often scenes from (by then) "classic" dramas or myths. We know from the Late Antique accounts of censorious Christian authors that Apollo's pursuit of Daphne (an episode in turn derived from Ovid's highly pictorial *Metamorphoses*) was a favorite of the genre. But virtually the entire range of hundreds of mythic tales seems to have been fair game, if not required for the professional pantomime performer. The second-century AD essayist Lucian prescribes a range of episodes for the dancer to learn, from the castration of Uranus, through the story of Prometheus, the birth of Dionysos, the abduction of Helen, the loves of Zeus, the fate of the daughters of Pandion, and the transfiguration of gods into beasts in Egyptian tales. "To sum it up, he will not be ignorant of anything that is told by Homer and Hesiod and the best poets, and above all by tragedy" (Lucian, *The Dance*, Ch. 61, trans. A. M. Harmon). The ideal pantomime dancer, it should be noted, was able to transform himself through gesture and movement from any one of these mythic characters into another, without losing the understanding and attention of his rapt audience.

Indeed, nearly every kind of myth, just as Lucian prescribed, was choreographed from the Renaissance through the nineteenth century. The output of one French choreographer, Pierre-Gabriel Gardel (1758–1840) offers a not untypical range of "ballet-pantomime" subjects: *Telemachus on Calypso's Isle* and *Psyche* (both 1790); *Bacchus and Ariadne* (1791); *Daphnis and Pandora* (1803); *Achilles on Scyros* (1804); *Venus and Adonis* (1808); *The Festival of Mars* (1809); *Vertumnus and Pomona* (after an Ovidian myth); and *Perseus and Andromeda* (both 1810).

At the same period, aristocratic ladies were experimenting with Greek-inspired dress designs and even private parties during which they would imitate poses and gestures from ancient depictions of mythic episodes. The infamous Lady Emma Hamilton (1765–1815), mistress of Lord Horatio Nelson and wife of Sir William Hamilton, the renowned collector of Greek vases, developed a series of such "attitudes" or "mimoplastic" imitations. In the guise of Medea, a Bacchant, Circe, and other mythic figures she was painted by several of the best portraitists of the era. Fads in dance, as well as fashion, rippled from her Neapolitan salon. This blend of antiquarianism, eroticism, and Romantic liberation resurfaced a century later when the San Francisco native, Isadora Duncan (1877–1927), adopting movements and gestures from Greek vases and sculptures she saw at the British Museum, danced flimsily clad and barefoot at London soirées (and afterwards, on the international stage). Both her freedom of "eurythmic" movement and fascination with ancient Greece affected subsequent American choreography. Her self-fashioning – Duncan described herself as "a battlefield where Apollo, Dionysos, Christ, Nietzsche, and Richard Wagner disputed the ground" – well represents the way myth was received via art, music, and philosophy at the end of the nineteenth century.

Its possibilities for representing a range of emotions from tenderness to violent passion made Classical myth a frequent vehicle for mid-twentieth-century choreographers. Martha Graham (1894–1991) retold the Minotaur story in a piece for two dancers, *Errand into the Maze* (1947), and the same year played the role of Jocasta in a Jung-inspired rendition of the Oedipus legend, *Night Journey* (1947). Her 1958 staging of the ballet *Clytemnestra* was a triumph, whereas her erotic *Phaedra* four years later drew shocked protests about the use of State Department funds for its European tour. Collaborating with the well-known sculptor and set designer Isamu Noguchi, she continued to make mythic dances, on such figures as Alcestis, Circe, and the Trojan Women (*Cortege of Eagles*, 1967) for decades thereafter.

VISUAL ART

Although both media have powerful visual components, dance and drama narrate their myths in time, through speech and song, gesture, and movement. Music, too, like poetry, is a temporal art. But painting and sculpture pose a different set of problems for the portrayal of myth. Rather than even begin to list the major artists who have depicted myths – from the Amasis Painter (sixth century BC) to Roy Lichtenstein (*Temple of Apollo*, 1964; *Laocoon*, 1988); Cy Twombly (*Proteus*, 1984) or Bracha L. Ettinger (e.g. the *Eurydice* series 1990–2009) – it is worth sketching three modes in which artists, ancient and modern, interact with the traditional tales.

First, they can create new versions. In visual art, this is harder than it sounds: while the dramatist can verbalize new names, situations, and settings, dropping an allusion to orient the theater-goer, the painter or sculptor must either retain enough signs of resemblance that his or her viewer will recall earlier depictions of Odysseus or Medea, Achilles or Hera, and make the connection; or must label the figures (something archaic Greek vase painters did often). A controversial case in point: an Athenian Red-figure cup discovered in 1834 and attributed to the Athenian painter Douris (c. 480 BC) shows in its interior the goddess Athena who watches as a huge serpent disgorges a man, alive. Behind them is a tree with a ram's skin in its branches. These clues assure us that the hero is Jason. The artist has also taken care to label him (the name is inscribed between his arms and long hanging hair). But in the hundreds of references to the Argonauts in ancient sources, not one mentions that the hero ever was swallowed by the dragon that guarded the Golden Fleece. Is it possible that Douris made up a new version, and if so, why? It has been suggested that Jason, in this otherwise unattested variant, undergoes the sort of near-death experiences that Odysseus, Heracles, and Orpheus endured on their journeying to the underworld. Comparatists will naturally adduce the Biblical story of Jonah in the whale. It is not impossible that Douris invented this striking detail, yet based it on his intuitions that Jason's story was a "multiform" – one sharing basic plot points – of other heroic quests.

The second mode of visual reception might be labeled "symbolic inclusion." For example, an Athenian vase now in Boston, from around 440 BC by the Lycaon Painter, illustrates an episode from the *Odyssey* as we have it. In Book 11 of the poem, Odysseus following Circe's instructions digs a pit for sacrificial animal blood and draws his sword to keep off the spirits who flock around to drink. Elpenor, his recently dead companion, emerges to explain that he had fallen, half-drunk, from a roof in Circe's palace and so made it to Hades' realm before his captain and crewmates arrived by ship. To the right of Odysseus, as he converses with the dead man (pit and animal carcasses between them) is Hermes – clearly identified by winged helmet and boots, carrying his herald's staff. And yet nowhere in the *Odyssey* episode does Hermes appear. What is going on?

The painter relies on the broader cultural knowledge of his audience, for whom Hermes is the conventional guide of souls into (and rarely from) the underworld. Also, in a different scene from the *Odyssey*, Hermes *did* assist Odysseus, giving him the magic root *moly*

Figure 5.1 Jason being disgorged by the dragon that guards the Golden Fleece, as Athena stands by. The Douris Painter (c. 475 BC) depicts a variant of the story attested nowhere else in antiquity, in which Jason apparently undergoes the sort of near-death experiences associated with Odysseus, Heracles, and Orpheus, or – more precisely – with the Biblical Jonah

Source: ART424807 Douris Painter (fifth century BC). Jason Disgorged by the Dragon with Athena. Kylix, from Cerveteri. Location: Museo Gregoriano Etrusco, Vatican Museums, Vatican Photo Credit: Universal Images Group/Art Resource, NY.

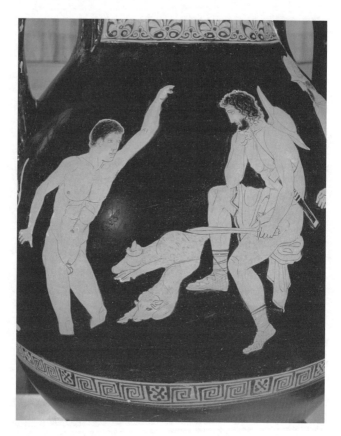

Figure 5.2 Odysseus and his recently deceased crew member Elpenor meeting
in the underworld, on an Attic Red-figure *pelike*, c. 440 BC. Although
in the surviving version of the Odyssey Hermes assisted in other
ways, he did not accompany Odysseus to the underworld. This
version of the myth by the Lykaon Painter creatively extrapolates
from a range of associations, seen in other stories, among the hero,
the god, and the site

Source: ART23606 Ulysses and Elpenor meeting in the underworld. Attic Red-figure
pelike, fifth century BC. Location: Museum of Fine Arts, Boston, USA, Photo Credit: Erich
Lessing/Art Resource, NY.

with which to overpower Circe in their first encounter. There may
even be a sly reference to the mythic tradition (unmentioned by
the epics) that Odysseus was the great-grandson of the god. In sum,

the painter includes Hermes because it "feels" right, symbolically, for the god to be in a familiar place and at the hero's side. (Also it makes a more pleasingly symmetrical painted composition.) One other motivation may have been symmetry with the other side of the vase, a regular concern for Greek painters who liked to make clever associations between a pot's two painted scenes. On the opposite side is depicted Poseidon, the sea-god who relentlessly pursues Odysseus, but who here is shown chasing the mortal Amymone by whom he will beget the sailor Nauplius. For purely compositional reasons, the god Hermes might be mirroring the appearance of his divine uncle in the other scene. Read more closely in conjunction, however, and with their associated myths in mind, the two scenes negotiate themes of god-hero antagonism, death and survival, and mastery over the sea.

If we want a modern parallel, a 1943 painting of Odysseus and Calypso by the German expressionist Max Beckmann is suggestive.

The two lovers recline in post-coital tenderness framed by a leopard-like creature, to the right, and on the left, an eagle. So far, the animals are a reasonable extrapolation based on the *Odyssey* description of the menagerie that surrounds the divine nymph's island home. But emerging from between the thighs of Odysseus and binding itself to his right shin (still sheathed in a greave) is a large snake. That, too, could be imagined as a member of Calypso's zoo. But given its multiplicity of associations in Greek and later myth and art (not to mention the positioning) it is difficult not to read the serpent symbolically. First, it materializes Calypso's erotic binding of her all-but-captive, Odysseus, who has spent seven years with her. Like the dragon-snake in the Jason vase, mentioned above, it summons up links with the heroic quest to slay monsters (but significantly is *part* of Odysseus himself here). Without getting too allegorical (see Chapter 1) we can interpret the painting as part of a long line of meditations, verbal and visual, on the voyage of Odysseus as representative of human emotional dilemmas.

A third mode of artistic interaction is the "catalogic." Knowing all the episodes in a hero's life, for instance, the painter might attempt to illustrate the series in one space. The Kodros Painter did just that with the deeds of Theseus shown inside a Red-figure cup (c. 440 BC). The hero drags a bull-headed man from a porch

Figure 5.3 "Ulysses and Calypso" by the German expressionist Max Beckmann
(1943) merges elements from the Odyssey episode with symbolically
suggestive animals (raptor, wildcat, snake) to create a mood both
pastoral and threatening. It captures the temptation to spend eternity
with a divinity rather than return to Ithaca

Source: ART374284 Beckmann, Max (1884–1950) © ARS, NY Ulysses and Calypso.
1943. Oil on canvas, 150 x 115.5 cm. Inv. 2887. Photo: Elke Walford. Location: Hamburger
Kunsthalle, Hamburg, Germany, Photo Credit: bpk, Berlin/Art Resource, NY.

(apparently of the labyrinth). Around this circular centerpiece are
seven encounters between Theseus and his nemeses on the road to
Athens (see Chapter 3) – Procrustes, Sinis, and the rest. An even

more ambitious "catalogue" is on the François Vase (now in Florence), a large mixing bowl (*krater*) from about 570 BC, signed by the painter Kleitias. Its profusion reminds us of the much later repertoire of the pantomime dancer (see above), but rather than being sequenced in time, all the mythic figures – more than 200 of them – are here visible almost at once. Many are identified by name. They include the heroes of the hunt for the Calydonian Boar (Peleus, Atalantê, et al.); Theseus leading the youths from Crete; the funeral games for Patroclus; the wedding of Peleus and Thetis; and the battle between the Centaurs and Lapiths.

This mode, while common in ancient wall paintings and early modern tapestries, is rarer in modern art, for good reason (to be discussed shortly). The painter of cryptic mythological scenes whom we just mentioned, Max Beckmann, also experimented with a form that seems to demand narrative connection – the "triptych," modeled on medieval three-section altarpieces. His *Argonauts* shows on its left panel an artist painting a near-naked Amazon-like woman who holds a sword; in the center, two young men, one crowned, one holding a parrot, are seemingly in conversation in front of an old man who emerges from the sea. A lyre lies on the ground. The right-hand panel contains another vignette of artistic processes, as four women play stringed or wind instruments. It is tempting to read the triptych not just as a narration but a *commemoration* of an event. The men in the middle are on the quest – they may be Jason and Orpheus (who accompanied the expedition), seeking advice from a sage. The painter and musicians who frame this central scene, with its stuff of raw adventure, could be performing in their own media renditions of the very tale enacted in the middle. In other words, the *Argonauts* becomes a sort of allegory and depiction of the very act of artistic reception that has brought us, over millennia, this myth. At the same time it is an excellent reminder that "receivers" like us are never passive – they have their own struggles and adventures, as well. The third artistic shaper of this triptych is, of course, not *in* the picture – Beckmann himself, who has crafted the whole. But his emphasis on depicting artists, right and left, forces us to think about his own role. Knowing that on December 27, 1950, the day after he completed this work, he died of a heart attack at the corner of 61st Street and Central Park West, we experience both epics in a new light.

FILM

Why are there so few "catalogic" works with their sequences of heroic careers? One easy answer for the modern period is: there are – in cinema. A sequence of action-packed frames, telling an epic story, in vivid visual details, trumps a static painting, even if it is multi-episodic. Moving pictures move us more.

Films, whether art-house or blockbuster, are undoubtedly among the most successful media at conveying ancient myth – especially the latter. These days, millions of people who never read the *Iliad* know about the Trojan War through Wolfgang Petersen's *Troy* (2004). The slender ancient epic by Apollonius of Rhodes has never had as many fans as the now classic *Jason and the Argonauts* (1963, directed by Don Chaffey, animation by Ray Harryhausen). *Clash of the Titans* (1981 – Harryhausen's last work), *Hercules* (action flick of 2014, Disney cartoon of 1997, or cult classic Arnold Schwarzenegger vehicle *Hercules in New York*, 1969), *Percy Jackson and the Olympians* (2010), and a score more have managed to interweave several strands of pop culture – young adult fiction, television specials, war movies, super-hero comics – showing, if nothing else, the amazing sturdiness of mythic plots. You know the basic motifs are hardwired into an audience's brain when parodies and meta-level movies can flourish – like Woody Allen's 1995 comedy *Mighty Aphrodite* (complete with tragic chorus) and the brilliant eight-minute *Oedipus* (2004) of Jason Wishnow, enacted entirely by stop-animated vegetables. (Spoiler alert: Oedipus is a potato with "eyes".)

These features of film, its wide popular appeal and reliance on the excellent visual memories of many audiences, make it the medium most like ancient Athenian drama. Just as an audience of the fifth-century comic playwright Aristophanes would "get" his fractured renditions of scenes from tragedies of his contemporary Euripides, so we appreciate each new *Hercules* as a take on all the previous movies. Intricate "intertextual" networks are constructed in this way, adding richness and depth to the experience of watching. Two myths that have undergone multiple treatments can illustrate this.

The story of Orpheus, as with opera, is made for film, since its themes – love, death, and music – make an enticing trio. Jean Cocteau dealt with the myth three times on film (and more in theater). *The Blood of a Poet* (1931) mixes trips to the underworld in a Parisian hotel with the Pygmalion motif (artist creates a living being) in a Surrealist extravaganza that nearly got its funder excommunicated. *Orpheus* (1950) features a protagonist who hears messages from a Rolls-Royce car radio and becomes obsessed with a princess of the underworld, which causes him to neglect his real-wife Eurydice. Cocteau's last film, the autobiographical *Testament of Orpheus*, merged the director with the mythic artist, now dying.

A year before, the brilliant *Black Orpheus* directed by Marcel Camus revivified the myth in modern times in a different venue, at *Carnaval* in Rio de Janeiro. The festival of disorder, music and dance provided a naturally surrealistic setting with some appropriate touches of ancient Greek Dionysian chaos in a *favela*. Each element of the myth, from the death of Eurydice to the murder of Orpheus, is carefully accounted for. Unlike Cocteau's treatments, dread and anxiety are built from *knowing* what will happen next (in the old tale) rather than from the shock of the totally unexpected (women melting into mirrors, and so forth). As with the visual reception of myth in painting, there are opportunities in film to manipulate both ignorance and awareness.

Odysseus naturally appeals to audiences on the level of adventure, with plenty of love interests, from nymphs to the hero's long-suffering wife Penelope. For film-makers it seems to parallel the Orpheus myth as a vehicle for examining their own artistic role (as Odysseus himself narrates most of his adventures in the *Odyssey*). The variety of female roles also makes it an interesting field for experimentation, social comment, and psychologizing of the myth. The otherwise straightforward adventure version, *Ulysses* (1954), starring Kirk Douglas, in a neat move casts Silvana Mangano as *both* Circe the sorceress who detains the homebound hero *and* his waiting wife Penelope. In this the director Mario Camerini seems to have picked up on a real feature of the original Greek poem. In the *Odyssey*, the use of formulaic phrases and type-scenes to describe various characters and situations does offer intriguing hints about the resemblances among goddesses and mortal women. For the audience, the question arises: what does Odysseus (Ulysses) really want, and does he get it?

The TV mini-series, *Homer's Odyssey* (1996) directed by Andrei Konchalovsky and gorgeously filmed in the Mediterranean, raises a problem for any representation of ancient myth: how to deal with the gods. The solutions are never satisfying since trying to capture the numinous (gauzy lighting effects, eyes that glow, deep voices) can be silly, while ignoring them altogether, or even cutting gods out of the action (as in *Troy*) misses an entire dimension of the verbal versions. One way around the dilemma is to re-imagine a plot like the *Odyssey* in modern terms, where gods are not expected to manifest themselves. *O Brother, Where Art Thou?* (2000) by Joel and Ethan Coen transposes the story of Ulysses (George Clooney) to the Depression-era South, in a madcap comic jaunt. Capturing something of the *Odyssey* hero, the film makes him a performer (a musician) as well as con-man, even suggesting that the two roles are inevitably related. The three-hour epic *Ulysses' Gaze* (1995) by the great Greek director Theo Angelopoulos makes explicit this sort of bond between artist and journeying hero. Harvey Keitel, the Odysseus figure, plays a filmmaker searching throughout the war-torn Balkans for early lost movies by two pioneering photographers. A post-modern vision of bombed-out Sarajevo, swathed in fog and haunted by classical music, underlines the sense of loss at the failed homecoming.

The best-known "remake" of the *Odyssey* story in the twentieth century, Joyce's novel *Ulysses* (mentioned above), formed the basis for Joseph Strick's 1967 film of the same name, and for *Bloom* (Sean Walsh, 2003). This mode – the filming of a pre-existing work of verbal art, rather than total re-casting of a mythic version – occupies a different point in the spectrum of reception. A number of excellent movies have represented original works by the Athenian tragedians. A trilogy of Euripidean dramas (*Electra, The Trojan Women, Iphigenia*) have been filmed by Michael Cacoyannis. Path-breaking productions by the Italian director Pier Paolo Pasolini of *Medea* (1970) and *Oedipus the King* (1967) ground the archaic myths in starkly primitive North African surroundings, thereby supporting some mid-century theorizing about the non-Greek sources of myth. This, too, is an important consideration for anyone interested in tracking receptions: how the artistic product can be inspired by scholarship. James Joyce professed a deep interest in Vico, and J. G. Frazer's *Golden Bough* affected mythic creations by Yeats, T. S. Eliot, John Millington Synge, and Joseph Conrad.

COMICS, GRAPHIC NOVELS, VIDEO GAMES

One of the many features that make these genres most interesting as receptors of myth is their cross-breeding. The high-end comic book series *300* by Frank Miller with Lynn Varley (1998, about the Battle of Thermopylae, admittedly ancient history rather than myth) took its inspiration from a 1962 movie, *The 300 Spartans* (a meditation, it now appears, on the Cold War conflict of East and West). In turn, Miller's book was adapted as a movie in 2006, with Miller's cooperation. The latter film intentionally copied the look and sequence of the intricate comic books. *Tomb Raider*, the video game, which occasionally uses Greek locations and gods in its play levels, made the leap to a movie version in 2001 (*Lara Craft Tomb Raider*), appropriately since the concept itself (a thrill-seeking hero-archaeologist) imitated the successful *Indiana Jones* franchise (based in turn on 1930s action-hero books). In the most desirable cases (commercially) a network of TV, websites, action figures, comics, and even amusement park rides will virally develop. It is useful to recall that a small-scale vision of this interaction was present in the ancient world, when poetry, song, dance, painting and even miniature figures of gods and heroes freely copied one another.

Given the frenzied pace of pop culture, the rise of comics about ancient mythic heroes half a century ago should make them items of antiquarian interest. But, in a way that recalls the continual evolution of Homeric epic, continuity with the past becomes a part of the richness of tale-telling. Competition with other tale-tellers adds to the complexity. DC Comics featured a Hercules figure in a Wonder Woman story as early as 1941. The hero made his first appearance in Marvel Comics in 1965, created by the famous Stan Lee. He is to this day one of the Avengers. *Hercules: Adventures of the Man-God* ran for only a brief stint, 1967–1969, but another limited run, *Hercules: The Thracian Wars* (Radical Comics) was chosen as the basis of the movie *Hercules* (2014), perhaps because its protagonist is a more nuanced and complex warrior. In the real comic universe, Superman predates the ancient Hercules, but his co-creator in the early 1930s, Jerry Siegel, has said that the Greek hero was a main inspiration for the Man of Steel. (The two got to clash in January, 1964 [Action Comics, No. 308] *Superman Meets the Goliath-Hercules!*)

More directly connected with the world of ancient myth is Wonder Woman, whose backstory makes her an Amazon princess, known as Princess Diana of Themyscira. She, too, not accidentally, dates from December 1941 when women began to enter the war effort en masse. With the Amazon tie-in, her creator, the psychologist William Moulton Marston (1893–1947) tapped into a fascination with the women warriors from the East reaching back to archaic Greece and extending through nineteenth-century theories about matriarchy and women's equality. Herodotus, the fifth-century BC historian, wrote of the Amazons' nomadic existence, skill with weapons, and eventual intermarriage with the Scythians, a large grouping of various populations on the Eurasian steppe. Since the 1990s, archaeological exploration of graves near the Kazakhstan border has confirmed the existence of tall, arrow-shooting warrior women (but not of a matriarchal society).

The motif of "Amazonomachy" (a fight with Amazons) can be seen on hundreds of ancient vases; Hippolyta, their queen, was an opponent of the Athenian hero Theseus. The comic book version of a battling Wonder Woman can be seen as an outgrowth, then, of ancient legend. In her latest incarnation, as drawn by Cliff Chiang with story by Brian Azzarello, Wonder Woman has morphed into a sophisticated feminist, fighting to protect the life of a single mother and her child.

The graphic novel has proven to be another ripe medium for mythic reception, with George O'Connor's *Olympian* series on individual divinities reaching best-seller status. *The Encyclopedia of Early Earth* (2013), a graphic novel by Isabel Greenberg, weaves Classical tales (e.g. the Cyclops) into a broader story deploying mythic motifs from a number of cultures. *Asterios Polyp* (2009) by David Mazzucchelli imports into its story of a washed-up Manhattan architect sequences related to Orpheus, Odysseus and even the "myth" of the first, round, four-legged, two-headed humans as told by Aristophanes in Plato's *Symposium*.

A similar range of strategies, from works devoted entirely to one figure, to mere allusions or even casual mythic ornamentation, can be found in Japanese *manga* (a popular traditional graphic art) and *anime* (animated stories often featuring adolescent heroes). Masami Kurumada's *Saint Seiya: Knights of the Zodiac* series (1986–90) centers on a reincarnation of Athena, who must do battle with Olympian foes. At least six *anime* films have sprung from it. Using a different strategy, of historical transposition, Riyoko Ikeda sets her young-adult love story *Window of Orpheus* (1975–81) in Germany and pre-Revolutionary Russia, using motifs like magic windows and mirrors reminiscent of the work of Cocteau. On the other end of the spectrum, *manga* writers can gesture toward a Classical figure, with no follow-through in terms of plot, suggesting at most a general resemblance. Hayao Miyazaki's *Nausicaä of the Valley of the Wind* (*manga* version 1982, *anime* 1984) stars a princess of the valley of the wind; the *Odyssey* has a princess with the same name; but the parallel seems to stop there. The *manga* heroine leads a fight to save civilization and cleanse her environmentally ruined dystopia of the future. In scope and development, she resembles more Princess Leia of the original *Star Wars* movie (1977), but with intriguing cosmic touches reaching back as far as Gilgamesh.

Finally, traditional tale-telling has taken on yet another life in the creation of video games. Classical myth is just another variety here, joining Tolkien-like warrior and wizard plots, Harry Potter spin-offs, and folklore from Japan, India, Persia and Egypt, and North America. A prime example is Sony Computer Entertainment's *God of War* (three installments for PlayStation, 2005–12). Written by David Jaffe, *GOW* tracks the career of a former Spartan general, Kratos (Greek for "power" and also the name of the henchman of Zeus appearing in Aeschylus' *Prometheus Bound*). Having signed over his life to Ares, Kratos is tricked into killing his own family (shades of Heracles); has to find Pandora's Box and its magic powers to defeat the war-god who is now attacking Athens; and gets to use his Blades of Power on a series of satisfyingly horrific Harpies, Gorgons, and Centaurs. Like Achilles, he can summon up the Rage of the Gods (as can a skilled player); like Perseus, he uses magic weapons (Medusa's gaze, the trident of Poseidon). Jaffe has acknowledged the inspiration of Ray Harryhausen films like *Clash of the Titans* (see above). As for why Classical myth appealed to him, Jaffe told an interviewer for the game-review website IGN: "monsters, heroes, love stories, gore, politics . . . what's not to love?" The history of myth reception proves him right.

FURTHER READING

On indigenous Roman myths, good starting points are T. P. Wiseman, *The Myths of Rome* (Exeter: University of Exeter Press, 2004) and J. N. Bremmer and N. M. Horsfall, *Roman Myth and Mythography* (London: Institute of Classical Studies, 1987). On the transmission of Greek myths to Rome, see Alan Cameron's *Greek*

Mythography in the Roman World (New York: Oxford University Press, 2004). For study of Ovid's pivotal role see *The Cambridge Companion to Ovid*, edited by Philip Hardie (Cambridge: Cambridge University Press, 2002) and *A Companion to Ovid*, edited by Peter Knox (Malden: Wiley-Blackwell, 2009).

The best introduction to the work of George Dumézil remains C. Scott Littleton's *The New Comparative Mythology*, 3rd edn (Berkeley: University of California Press, 1982). Dumézil's own *Archaic Roman Religion* (Chicago: University of Chicago Press, 1970) summarizes his theses. Roger Woodard, *Indo-European Sacred Space: Vedic and Roman Cult* (Champaign: University of Illinois Press, 2006) re-examines these with new investigations.

On reception of myth in general invaluable lists of artists and works are in Jane Reid (ed.), *The Oxford Guide to Classical Mythology in the Arts: 1300–1990s* (Oxford: Oxford University Press, 1993). Context is provided in *A Companion to Classical Receptions*, edited by Lorna Hardwick and Christopher Stray (Malden: Wiley-Blackwell, 2008), in a series of fine case studies. Further recent bibliography can be found in Pura Nieto Hernández, *Mythology: Oxford Bibliographies Online Research Guide* (Oxford: Oxford University Press, 2010) and William Hansen, *Classical Mythology: A Guide to the Mythical World of the Greeks and Romans* (Oxford: Oxford University Press, 2004). Detailed essays, in English (but with mostly German bibliography) are in *Brill's New Pauly Supplements I – Volume 4: The Reception of Myth and Mythology*, edited by Maria Moog-Grünewald and Giorgio Baruchello (Leiden: Brill, 2010).

Useful for approaching literary reception are Douglas Bush, *Mythology and the Renaissance Tradition in English Poetry* (revised edn, New York: Norton, 1963); Theodore Ziolkowski, *Ovid and the Moderns* (Ithaca: Cornell University Press, 2005); Jane Chance, *Medieval Mythography, vol 1: From Roman North Africa to the School of Chartres, AD 433–1177* (Gainesville: University Press of Florida, 1994) and *vol. 2, From the School of Chartres to the Court at Avignon, 1177–1350* (Gainesville: University Press of Florida, 2000); and Charles Martindale (ed.), *Ovid Renewed: Ovidian Influences on Literature and Art from the Middle Ages to the Twentieth Century* (Cambridge: Cambridge University Press, 1990).

Gilbert Highet's *The Classical Tradition: Greek and Roman Influences on Western Literature* (Oxford: Oxford University Press, 1949) is still reliable. For reception of one resilient figure, see W. B. Stanford, *The Ulysses Theme: A Study in the Adaptability of a Traditional Hero*, 2nd edn (Ann Arbor: University of Michigan Press, 1968).

On drama, see Fiona Macintosh, "Tragedy in Performance: Nineteenth- and Twentieth-Century Productions," in *The Cambridge Companion to Greek Tragedy*, edited by Patricia E. Easterling (Cambridge: Cambridge University Press, 1996). For lyric poems, an excellent anthology is *Gods and Mortals: Modern Poems on Classical Myths*, edited by Nina Kossman (New York: Oxford University Press, 2001). Analysis of work up to mid-century is provided in *Ancient Myth in Modern Poetry* by Lillian Feder (Princeton: Princeton University Press, 1971). Peter Dronke, *Medieval Latin and the Rise of the European Love-Lyric*, 2nd edn (Oxford: Oxford University Press, 1968) is a groundbreaking study. On fantasy prose, see *Classical Traditions in Science Fiction*, edited by Brett Rogers and Benjamin Stevens (Oxford: Oxford University Press, 2015).

The Ancient Dancer in the Modern World, edited by Fiona Macintosh (Oxford: Oxford University Press, 2010) is a fine collection of essays and further reading suggestions, while a good bibliography on music can be found in "Classical Myth in Music: A Selective List," by Donald Poduska, in *The Classical World* (92), 1999: 195–276.

The mythic heritage of visual art is enormous. Since ancient images can themselves be treated as receptions, see first Klaus Junker, *Interpreting the Images of Greek Myths: an Introduction* (Cambridge: Cambridge University Press, 2012). Also valuable are Thomas Carpenter, *Art and Myth in Ancient Greece* (London: Thames & Hudson, 1991) and H. Alan Shapiro, *Myth into Art: Poet and Painter in Classical Greece* (London: Routledge, 1994). For later periods, Philip Mayerson provides a start in *Classical Mythology in Literature, Art, and Music* (Newburyport: Focus, 2001). See also Malcolm Bull, *The Mirror of the Gods: Classical Mythology in Renaissance Art* (London: Penguin, 2005). A classic study is Jean Seznec's *The Survival of the Pagan Gods* (Princeton: Princeton University Press, 1981). The vast *Lexicon Iconographicum Mythologiae Classicae (LIMC)* (Zürich: Artemis & Winkler, 1981–1999) provides information on all known ancient images.

On film, the most up-to-date resource is Martin Winkler's online Oxford Bibliography *Classics and Cinema*. Winkler has also edited *Classical Myth and Culture in the Cinema* (New York: Oxford University Press, 2001).

A reliable survey volume on myth in comics, graphic novels, video games and other popular formats has yet to be written. The journal *Games and Culture* (Sage) is a good resource. *International Journal of the Classical Tradition* (Springer) and *Classical Receptions* (Oxford) frequently look beyond strictly literary or high cultural forms.

On Amazons, see Adrienne Mayor, *The Amazons: Lives and Legends of Warrior Women across the Ancient World* (Princeton: Princeton University Press, 2014). And on the comic book Amazon queen, see Jill Lepore, *The Secret History of Wonder Woman* (New York: Knopf, 2014).

INDEX

Euripides 19, 26, 32, 35, 74–5, 80–1,
  101, 139, 158
Europa 128
Eurystheus 62, 80, 91, 93

Fates 25, 48
flamen 137
flood myth 26, 57, 66, 85
François Vase 157
Frazer, James George 90, 121–5, 131,
  160
Freud, Sigmund 110–16, 129

Gaia 42, 58, 112; *see also* Earth
Genesis 40, 42–3, 61, 63, 65
Giants 47
Gorgon 11, 20, 27, 48, 84–7, 163

Hades 2, 26, 49, 56, 80, 93, 135, 148,
  152
Harpies 86, 163
Harrison, Jane Ellen 123–5, 131
Hecataeus of Miletus 25–6
Helen 5, 32, 60–1, 66, 77, 107, 150
Helios 60, 63, 75
Hephaestus 17, 26, 28, 52, 55, 64, 135
Hera 28, 49, 56, 62, 73, 75, 79, 91–3,
  135, 152
Heracles 11–12, 15, 17, 25–6, 35,
  48–9, 51, 62, 64, 68, 76, 79–80,
  85, 90–98, 102, 105, 107–9, 143,
  152–3, 163
Heraclitus of Ephesus 23
Hermes 28, 35, 51, 55, 64, 84, 135,
  148, 153–5
herms 64
Herodotus 10, 14, 19, 25–6, 35, 61,
  71, 120, 125, 141, 162
hêrôs 69–70, 75–6
Hesiod 1, 13, 23–4, 29–35, 47–61,
  65 6, 75 6, 101, 112, 116–19, 125,
  129, 135, 150

Hesperides 48, 93, 108
Hippothon 9
historiê 141
Hittites 57–9, 137
Hundred–Handers 47–9
Hyacinthus 63
Hydra 49, 93
Hygieia 79
Hypsipyle 87

Iliad 4, 13, 24, 28, 31–2, 35, 37, 66, 75,
  77, 86, 143, 145, 158
Indo–European 59–61, 66, 88, 137–8,
  164
initiation 18, 44, 66, 86, 93, 97, 99
Iphicles 61
Iphigenia 63, 81–2, 101, 149, 160
Isles of the Blessed 76; *see also* Elysian
  Fields
Itys 20–1, 145

Jason 20, 35, 75, 84–90, 93, 99, 101,
  152–3, 155, 157–8
Juno 113, 135
Jupiter 109, 135–7, 143

katasterism 105
Kleitias 157
Kleomedes 74
Klotho 48
Kodros Painter 155
Korinthos 12
Kronos 9, 27, 34, 47–50, 55, 58, 113

Lachesis 48
Laertes 85
Laius 85
Lévi–Strauss, Claude 128, 132
Linus 92
Livy 136–8
logos 28, 33, 83
Lucan 142